JESUS

LISA HARPER

JESUS

A Scandalously Devoted, Conspicuously Uncool, Super-Transparent Homage to Who Our Savior Is and How Much He Loves Us

DEVOTIONAL

B&H
PUBLISHING
BRENTWOOD, TENNESSEE

978-1-0877-7819-8

Published by B&H Publishing Group
Brentwood, Tennessee

Dewey Decimal Classification: 242.64
Subject Heading: DEVOTIONAL LITERATURE
/ JESUS CHRIST / MEDITATIONS

Cover design and handlettering by Tim Green at FaceOut
Studio. Author photo by Amy Conner Photography.

1 2 3 4 5 6 7 • 27 26 25 24 23

This devotional is dedicated to the beautiful sisterhood of women who've been coming to our neighborhood Bible study at Belle's for the past fourteen years. Leaning into Jesus with y'all every Tuesday morning is an incredible joy and privilege. It's also been such a sweet and necessary anchor for my rolling stone kind of life. Thank you.

ACKNOWLEDGMENTS

I'm again indebted to Ashley Gorman, my brilliant editor at B&H who is both gracious and gifted. She goes far above and beyond the call of duty to smooth out most of my rough literary edges! I'm also deeply appreciative for all my professors in the doctoral program at Denver Seminary but none more so than my mentor/big brother, Dr. Jim Howard, who continues to generously pour his hard-earned theological wisdom into the cupped hands of my heart and mind.

CONTENTS

INTRODUCTION

MY DAUGHTER MISSY (YOU'LL hear a lot about her in this devotional if you don't already know her story!) turned thirteen this past year and her passage into pre-adulthood came complete with her first crush. Of course, my lips will remain zipped about exactly who this young man is because all her secrets are safe with me (well, at least until her rehearsal dinner at which point all the romantic fodder from her youth will be fair game for a video montage!). But what I can divulge is that he's a good kid and Missy is momentarily riveted by the contours of his story!

I was sitting across the table from her recently, listening to her wax poetic about who he walked into school with, what he wore that day, when he bumped into her in the hallway (after she "accidentally" stepped into his path!), where he sat while eating his peanut butter and jelly sandwich with the crusts cut off at lunch, and why oh why he and his family don't attend our church or live in a neighborhood closer to ours. I couldn't help smiling over the sweet innocence of her preoccupation, but I also found myself musing, "Goodness gracious, I want to be *at least* as preoccupied with Jesus as my girl is with that skinny little dude."

I want to know who's on Jesus's mind, what He likes to talk about, when His voice gets animated, where He's prone to linger and have long conversations, and why He didn't turn James and John into pillars of salt when those oblivious goofballs brazenly asked if they could flank either side of His future throne (Mark 10:35–45)! I want to know who makes His divine eyes twinkle, what causes the corners of His mouth to curve into a smile, when He doubles over with laughter, where His heart sings for joy, and why He cried outside Lazarus's tomb—was it over His dear friend's death or Mary and Martha's lack of faith that He would ultimately raise him from the dead (John 11:35)? I want to know who else made Him sad, what else prompted tears to roll down His incarnate cheeks, where He went when He needed to grieve alone, and since He's perfectly God why Jesus chose to "learn" obedience through suffering (Heb. 5:8). I want to know what He would describe as the highest mountains and the lowest valleys of His earthly ministry. I want to sample my Savior's favorite foods, listen to His favorite music, and take in His favorite views with my own eyes. I want to know everything I possibly can about our Redeemer because He is *the Love of my life*—my forever crush!

I've been a Christ-follower for fifty-plus years. I've been in vocational ministry for thirty-plus years. I've spent over a decade studying God and His Word in seminary at both the master's and doctoral level. I've filled in more Bible study blanks than there are stripes on a huge herd of zebras. But I still feel like I've only scratched the surface of knowing Jesus. He is infinitely more interesting than we can wrap our finite minds around; and no matter what new season we enter, it seems like His attributes are *always better*—more compassionate, more accessible, more righteous, more empathetic—than the first, second, third, or thousandth time we encounter them!

No matter where you are in your walk of faith (some of you have known Jesus longer and enjoy a more intimate relationship with Him than I do, while some of you aren't sure that He's anything more than an existential construct and you're not yet convinced He's actually *knowable*), my hope is that while traveling with me on this sixty-day adventure, you'll find yourself leaning more fully into the outstretched arms of our Messiah . . . maybe for the very first time.

And so, as you go on that journey, here are a few things to expect in the terrain along the way:

1. For every day's devotional experience (there are sixty days total), you'll enjoy a passage of Scripture to consider, usually a little humor (because who doesn't need to laugh every now and then in the crazy times we're in?), and some theological nuggets (because I just can't help myself when it comes to sharing tidbits of transformational information I've learned along the path of walking with Jesus for half a century!).

2. Another thing to note is that each day of this devotional centers on either something Jesus *is* for us, or something Jesus *does* in the Scriptures (and in our lives!). Which basically just means I'm purposefully trying to focus our attention on either the *person* of Jesus or the *work* of Jesus—because when you come into contact with those two elements of who He is, you'll never be the same!

3. And last, expect a lot of stories with my daughter, Missy, as a major character. She's been the apple of my eye ever since I started the

process of adopting her from Haiti shortly after her first mother's death in 2012, and God continues to teach me through her every single day.

All that being said, let's dive into Jesus. Because He's not only central to the Bible's story—He's central to the world's story and to *your* story, as I prayerfully hope you'll see by the end of your journey through this book. And it's a good thing to have Him smack dab in the center of your life; because when Jesus is at the center, everything else falls into place.

Love,
Lisa

Day 1

JESUS IS TOTALLY SCANDAL-WORTHY

Then one of the Pharisees invited him to eat with him. He entered the Pharisee's house and reclined at the table. And a woman in the town who was a sinner found out that Jesus was reclining at the table in the Pharisee's house. She brought an alabaster jar of perfume and stood behind him at his feet, weeping, and began to wash his feet with her tears. She wiped his feet with her hair, kissing them and anointing them with the perfume. When the Pharisee who had invited him saw this, he said to himself, "This man, if he were a prophet, would know who and what kind of woman this is who is touching him—she's a sinner!" LUKE 7:36–39

———————————

I'VE BEEN IN CHURCH since I was in utero. Which means I've heard most of the Bible stories many, many times. Plus, I was raised partly in the Baptist tradition, which means I've seen most of them flannel-graphed! I've also had eight years of masters—and doctoral-level seminary training. The bottom line is: I'm no stranger to the Scriptures. But here's the deal, y'all—God's Word isn't a flat, one-dimensional text that we can memorize and effectively "conquer." It's a supernatural love story with more facets than our finite human minds can possibly master. No matter how many times you hear, read, or peruse a biblical passage, there are *always* new truths to glean and contours to explore!

I recently heard our seminary president, Dr. Mark Young of Denver Seminary, preach on a familiar passage, and I was blown away by a poignant detail I've missed for decades. He unpacked the story in Luke about a woman who washed Jesus's feet with her tears, dried them with her hair, then anointed them with perfumed oil. He explained how every Gospel account includes an encounter where Jesus was anointed by a woman (Matt. 26:6–13, Mark 14:3–9, Luke 7:36–50, and John 12:1–8). He shared that of these four encounters recorded in the Gospels, New Testament scholars agree that there are at least two separate anointings going on in these scenes, based on the chronological differences and unique characteristics in the individual narratives.

Furthermore, John's account specifies that the "anointer" was Lazarus's dear sister, Mary of Bethany, who was a good girl, despite the fact that she chose to chill at Jesus's feet instead of crushing it in the kitchen like her super-productive sibling, Martha! Yet Luke's account refers to the woman anointing Jesus as a "sinner" (which commentators say is a euphemism for a prostitute), who was neither a good girl nor a personal friend of the Christ like Mary of Bethany. Instead, the woman in Luke's Gospel account was likely one of several uninvited guests who'd gathered in Simon's yard to lean against the wall of the courtyard and eavesdrop on the alfresco conversation and/or beg for food, as was common in the Ancient Near East.

As I read about her in Luke 7, I can't help but wonder what compelled her to come. Maybe she'd watched Christ engage with a grieving widow who was trudging alongside the pallbearers carrying her dead son's body and looked on in awe as He raised the boy back to life because that miraculous encounter happens just prior to hers in Luke 7. Some teachers think she put her hope in Jesus through the ministry of John the Baptist. Whatever the case, this sinful woman was willing to ignore propriety, invite judgment, and initiate a scandal to get closer to Him.

According to tradition, Jesus and the other fellas (formal meals at that time were segregated by gender) reclined on cushions while they ate because tables in that era were low-slung—more like a rustic coffee table than our modern dining tables. They would've leaned on their left elbows and eaten with their right hands because Torah depicted the right hand as superior to the left and, therefore, was considered the "clean" hand (Gen. 48:13–14; Lev. 7:32; 1 Kings 2:19; Ps. 17:7; Eccles. 10:2). And their feet would've been extended behind them because feet were considered the dirtiest part of the body, and so, naturally, a Jew would've been diligent about keeping those yucky tootsies as far away from the food as possible.

These first-century facets clarify why Luke describes this woman as coming from *behind* Jesus to wash and anoint His soon-to-be-pierced feet. Her tears made fetching a basin of water unnecessary and there was no need for a towel either because she used her hair to dry them. The hair thing is no small detail here (and was sure to make some observers of her demonstrative devotion gasp) because, as you probably already know, women in New Testament culture rarely let their hair down apart from private settings with their husbands. To have free-flowing hair back then was perceived as a very intimate gesture. Which is why Simon started acting priggish and presumed something to the effect of: "If this dude was really a prophet or even a relatively astute rabbi, he would've realized this chick is trashy and would've removed his feet from her filthy hands!"

I imagine Simon rolling his eyes and huffing indignantly when she continued her consecration with a kiss and then sealed it by rubbing our Redeemer's feet with expensive perfumed oil instead of the standard olive oil that was normally used for anointing (which would've been her most valuable possession if she was indeed a "lady of the evening" as many theologians assert). Based on Simon's mental recoil and ancient protocol, her actions were utterly scandalous.

But Jesus wasn't offended. In fact, He praised her affectionate attentiveness and chastised Simon's lack thereof. Which is the point in the text we get to the marvelous minutia that blew fresh faith into my sails recently:

> *Turning to the woman*, he said to Simon . . . (Luke 7:44a, emphasis mine)

That petite phrase paints a glorious portrait of grace. Because while Jesus reproved this rude religious leader who was oblivious to the fact that *God Himself in the flesh* was his dinner party guest, He was gazing compassionately at the woman Simon dismissed. She was used to men looking at her with lust in their eyes, but our Savior's unconditionally loving focus was surely unprecedented. Can't you picture her tipping that alabaster jar upside down and thumping it with the heel of her hand in response, intent on giving Him every last drop of her adoration?

Propriety is a small price to pay when compared with the invaluable gift of divine redemption.

- **WHAT'S THE MOST** extravagant gift you've proverbially laid at the feet of Jesus?

- **HAVE YOU EVER** been accused of being too excessive in your devotion to Him? If so, did their chagrin dampen your zeal?

- **IF IT'S BEEN** a while since you felt as devoted to Jesus as this woman, explore why. What do you think is contributing to your lack of affection for Him?

JESUS IS PERFECTLY DIVINE

The Jews surrounded him and asked, "How long are you going to keep us in suspense? If you are the Messiah, tell us plainly." "I did tell you and you don't believe," Jesus answered them. "The works that I do in my Father's name testify about me. But you don't believe because you are not of my sheep. My sheep hear my voice, I know them, and they follow me. I give them eternal life, and they will never perish. No one will snatch them out of my hand. My Father, who has given them to me, is greater than all. No one is able to snatch them out of the Father's hand. <u>I and the Father are one</u>." JOHN 10:24–30, EMPHASIS MINE

WAY BACK IN 2004, long before grown people began pulling hamstrings trying to keep up on the latest social media app or overgrown people began making themselves miserable on Keto (mostly teasing but true from my own half-starved vantage point!), an epic Hollywood blockbuster called *The Passion of the Christ* came to theaters and captured the imaginations of millions of moviegoers. It ultimately grossed more than 600 million dollars with its dramatic portrayal of the life, death, and resurrection of Jesus. It also catapulted the handsome young actor who played the Messiah, Jim Caviezel, to seemingly overnight stardom. A few months after the movie hit theaters, several of my girlfriends attended a large conference where Christian publishers, record labels, and the then-budding faith-based film industry met with ministry, retail, radio, and television representatives to promote their upcoming projects. And much to their delight, Mr. Caviezel was there in person.

I had dinner with a few of them soon after they got home from the conference, and when I asked what upcoming books, Bible studies, or worship recordings they were really excited about, they drew a blank. Neither remembered much at all about the hundreds of faith-based projects they'd been pitched. But honey, they'd become experts on Jim Caviezel because they'd spent the bulk of the two-day conference trying to figure out where he was at any given moment and then, when they located their poor prey, they followed him around the convention floor like starstruck paparazzi! While describing their mission/mild stalking in detail to me, one sighed dreamily and said, "Oh Lisa, if you'd been there, you would've traipsed after him too because that Jesus was absolutely *gorgeous!*" I couldn't help laughing—and they good-naturedly poked fun at themselves—that they were swooning over a man named Jim who'd simply pretended to be Jesus.

I don't think there's anything wrong with their momentary crush, although I do think it underscores humanity's tendency to dumb down our Messiah's divinity. To rub the shine off His proverbial crown a bit so we won't be as intimidated by that whole "divine nature" thing He has going on. Associating Him with an attractive actor isn't much different than referring to Him by anthropomorphic (which is a fancy word that, in the context of theology, means using human attributes to describe God) terms like *copilot* or *homeboy*; it's simply a way to lower our perceived drawbridge around the King of all kings so that we, as commoners, can access Him. Which, again, in and of itself isn't necessarily a bad or heretical habit. Heck, the accessibility of Jesus is a recurring theme throughout the New Testament!

We just need to be careful not to throw the proverbial supernatural baby out with the relevant bathwater because the undiluted deity of Jesus Christ is a big deal. After all, when historic Christianity was being built at the *very* start of the church era, the undiluted deity of Jesus Christ was (and still is) one of the foundational walls. From the very beginning of the formation of the Christian belief system, the fact that Jesus has a divine nature—that He's really, truly *God* in the flesh—is and always has been a nonnegotiable. In fact, the divinity of Jesus was so imperative to our faith that it was the main focus of the first two Christian councils when the need for orthodox boundaries became apparent. Why? Because in the late (AD) 200s and early 300s, church leaders became aware of Gnostic mystery cults and errant teachings that were being circulated about Jesus; namely, that He was of a lesser nature than God the Father. In other words, some heretical yahoos had infiltrated first-century Christian circles and were talking smack about Jesus, which was causing confusion among believers.

In response, Emperor Constantine called church leaders together for the first formal Christian council in Nicaea in AD 325 to prayerfully consider two main questions: *How does this teaching stack up against the whole of what Scripture teaches?* and *What are the implications of this teaching regarding our salvation through Jesus?* Ultimately, the Council of Nicaea concluded that Jesus's divine nature was the very nature of God, and that He was, in fact, *Immanuel*, God with us.

One of my all-time favorite Christian scholars, authors, professors, and pretend theological boyfriends, Dr. J. I. Packer, eloquently elaborated on this magnificent mystery with this observation:

> The really staggering Christian claim is that Jesus of Nazareth was God made man—that the second person of the Godhead became the "second man" (1 Cor. 15:47), determining human destiny, the second representative head of the race, and that he took humanity without the loss of deity, so that Jesus of Nazareth was as truly divine as he was human.[1]

He took humanity without the loss of deity . . . that'll make you think twice before putting one of those "Jesus is my homeboy" bumper stickers on your car, won't it?

- **THINK ABOUT OUR** modern habit of using anthropomorphic/casual terms for Jesus like *copilot* and *homeboy.* In what ways has this dulled our awe about the fact that Jesus is divine?

- **IN WHAT SPECIFIC** ways do you sometimes treat Jesus like He's just a man, and not God? What are some practical ways to restore appropriate reverence and awe (not formality or rigidity, mind you!) into your real, intimate *relationship* with Jesus?

Day 3
JESUS IS ALSO PERFECTLY HUMAN

Jacob's well was there, and Jesus, <u>worn out from his journey,</u> sat down at the well. It was about noon. JOHN 4:6, EMPHASIS MINE

When Jesus saw her crying, and the Jews who had come with her crying, <u>*he was deeply moved in his spirit and troubled.*</u> *"Where have you put him?"* he asked. "Lord," they told him, "come and see." <u>*Jesus wept.*</u> JOHN 11:33–35, EMPHASIS MINE

Adopt the same attitude as that of Christ Jesus, who, existing in the form of God, did not consider equality with God as something to be exploited. Instead he emptied himself by assuming the form of a servant, taking on the likeness of humanity. PHILIPPIANS 2:5–7B

HAVE YOU EVER BEEN driving down a road during a rainstorm, and noticed a big body of water gathered to one side of the road—one that you're sure you'll hydroplane on if you don't have enough time to swivel the wheels around the puddle? We've all been there, and we've all probably thought the exact same words: *Avoid catastrophe!* Problem is, when we dart our wheels away from the puddle, sometimes we overcorrect, sending our car into another type of potential danger. Often there's a ditch on the other side of the road awaiting us, and if we're not careful, we'll drive our car straight into that parallel catastrophe on the other side of the road—even if it was for good reason. Overcorrecting from one sort of danger can sometimes lead us into another sort that's equally disastrous.

If that's ever happened to you, don't worry. You're not alone. Almost everyone overcorrects at some point, Christians and non-Christians alike. In fact, you could say church history is one course-correction after the other, swinging to and fro to avoid catastrophe, which oftentimes led to overcorrecting.

Just over one hundred years after the matter of Jesus's divinity was conclusively settled at the First Council of Nicaea, another formal meeting of Christian leaders convened at the Council of Chalcedon in AD 451. Why another council? What else could possibly need to be settled? Well, an "overcorrection" took place after Nicaea. People were convinced about Jesus being God, which is great, but the pendulum had swung so far in that direction that a new theory had emerged: namely, that Jesus was fully divine but wasn't fully human. One leader who held this unorthodox view went so far as to insist that when Jesus cried at the tomb of Lazarus, they were faux tears—the tears of an actor![2] Here we have a quintessential example of driving into one theological catastrophe in order to avoid another. Ultimately, the Council of Chalcedon affirmed that Jesus Christ has two natures; that He was and is truly divine *and* truly human at the same time, that we don't have to give up one in order to affirm the other. In short, this is the point in history where God's people learned how to avoid the puddle *and* the ditch when it came to who Jesus really is.

This whole history lesson is why we now call Jesus "God incarnate." He's fully God, but *incarnated* as a human. Or, as I said before, Christ is truly divine *and* truly human at the same time. Granted that's a mouthful and a mind-full. I think it's even more difficult than playing Twister at my age to wrap our human cognition around the fact that Jesus is perfectly divine and perfectly human at the same time! But leave it to my academic crush whom I introduced you to yesterday, Dr. J. I. Packer, to further elucidate this truth for us:

> It is here, in the thing that happened at the first Christmas, that the profoundest and most unfathomable depths of the Christian revelation lie. "The Word became flesh" (John 1:14); God became man; the divine Son became a Jew; the Almighty appeared on earth as a helpless human baby, unable to do more than lie and stare and wriggle and make noises, needing to be fed and changed and taught to talk like any other child. And there was no illusion or deception in this; the babyhood of the Son of God was a reality. The more you think about it, the more staggering it gets. Nothing in fiction is so fantastic as is the truth of the Incarnation.[3]

I wholeheartedly agree . . . the more I think about the King of all kings humbly condescending to wear an ancient pair of Pampers, the more gobsmacked I get! As an adult rabbi, all Jesus did was speak and the wind and waves obeyed Him (Mark 4:35–41). All He did was touch a leper and the disfiguring disease immediately left the poor man (Matt. 8:1–4). All He did was walk up to a commotion taking place on a spooky tombstone-strewn hill called the Gerasenes, where a legion of demons was tormenting a man, and His mere presence caused that evil gang of satan's[4] minions to have a conniption fit because they recognized His supernatural supremacy (Mark 5:1–13). Yet, before King Jesus chose to express His divine power and majesty, He stooped to be potty-trained, to learn Aramaic (the New Testament sayings of Jesus are typically recorded in Greek, but His native tongue was Aramaic—more specifically, a Galilean version of western Aramaic—although Luke 4:16–20 reveals that He also read and spoke Hebrew[5]), to do His chores, and eventually to saunter down a dirt road to school like all the other little boys in Nazareth.

He really was fully God and fully man at the same time. And that miraculous reality of what supersmart theology people call the "hypostatic union" is why the author of Hebrews could describe Jesus as our *empathetic* High Priest:

> Therefore, since we have a great high priest who has ascended into heaven, Jesus the Son of God, let us hold firmly to the faith we profess. For we do not have a high priest who is unable to empathize with our weaknesses, but we have one who has been tempted in every way, just as we are—yet he did not sin. Let us then approach God's throne of grace with confidence, so that we may receive mercy and find grace to help us in our time of need. (Heb. 4:14–16 niv)

If you and I could understand, even in part, just how much this passage conveys about our Savior's deep understanding of our human experience, if we could but remember that this Scripture means our Savior can say, "Been there, done that!" with regards to every single emotion in the human continuum—including our deepest grief and most difficult struggles—it would dramatically increase our security as His stumbling saints. Jesus is not some faraway, dispassionate, untouchable, cape-wearing superhero who redeems us from a distance, y'all! Instead, He's an up-close, incarnate, compassionate Redeemer who intimately relates to every, single, thing we've been through or are afraid of going through.

Marinate for a moment in the juxtapositional miracle of Jesus's *divine humanity*, and I bet you'll find yourself leaning more fully into His embrace. Because since He's capable of knowing us completely, His love is surely unconditional.

- **REREAD HEBREWS 4:14–16.** What phrase is the most meaningful to you and why?

- **WHAT PERSONAL "WEAKNESS"** do you most need Jesus to empathize with this season?

- **IN WHAT WAYS** do you treat Jesus as if He's only divine, but not human? What do you miss out on when you forget about His human nature?

Day 4

JESUS IS A PRESENT AND
PASSIONATE BRIDEGROOM

"I will not leave you as orphans; I am coming to you. In a little while the world will no longer see me, but you will see me. Because I live, you will live too. On that day you will know that I am in my Father, you are in me, and I am in you. The one who has my commands and keeps them is the one who loves me. And the one who loves me will be loved by my Father. <u>I also will love him and will reveal myself to him</u>." JOHN 14:18–21, EMPHASIS MINE

Let us be glad, rejoice, and give him glory, because the marriage of the Lamb has come, and <u>his bride has prepared herself</u>. REVELATION 19:7, EMPHASIS MINE

NOT LONG AGO A friend lectured me about the lack of direction in my love life. I think it was her way of saying the lack of a pulse, since my dating life hasn't registered a blip on the romantic radar in years. Anyway, she strongly encouraged me to join an online dating service. I thought, *So, it's come down to this.*

I know finding the love of your life via the Internet has become commonplace in our culture; I've seen the advertisements featuring cute couples gazing at each other in adoration, so it obviously works for some people. But it still feels a tad awkward to me. Not as desperate as renting a plane to fly a *1-800-588- please help Lisa get a date*, but awkward, nonetheless.

My friend argued that the main reason I was hesitant about collaborating with a high-tech matchmaker was my pride. And since pride has certainly been my downfall before, her logic made sense. I thought, *Maybe she's right. Maybe I should just get over myself and give it a try.* So I paid for a three-month trial membership to a Christian online dating service.

Let's just say I should have followed my initial instincts. I won't take the time to enumerate all the "date-astrophes" I had as a result of that digital dating adventure. I'll just share the highlights/lowlights of one because I think it'll give you the gist of the entire experience. There was a particular gentleman who was witty and personable and even used spell-check in our email conversations, which is quite charming to me because good grammar is more important than broad shoulders in my estimation. Plus, he was gainfully employed and did not live in his mother's basement. These aren't necessarily nonnegotiables for me when it comes to gentleman callers, but let's just call them "strong preferences."

So anyway, between his humor, grammatical skills, and his full-time job, I got my hopes up and we began making plans to meet face-to-face. Which is when he sent me a lengthy message explaining why he'd never posted a picture on his profile because, while he was gainfully employed, his work was actually entirely online due to his severe social anxiety and hesitancy to leave his house—even for a few hours—out of concern for how his absence could negatively affect the emotional security of the *dozens* of pet cats he'd adopted over the years.

Now, please hear me. I'm not saying there's a single thing wrong with being a homebody with feline companions—heck, I'm a middle-aged woman who likes going to the local tractor wholesale supply store! However, I'm an extrovert who travels for a living and has a daughter who's allergic to cats, so I thought I should probably go ahead and graciously bow out of this whole ordeal before I met this guy since there likely wasn't any long-term potential. Of course, I didn't want to hurt his feelings, so I prayed and pondered how to best communicate the end of our not-quite-started-yet relationship without bumming him out too much, and decided I'd send him a reply later on that evening.

At this point my plan probably sounds well and good to you, but there's a detail I have not divulged until right now. Unfortunately, I wasn't my normal self that night because my doctor had put me on antibiotics and a strong steroid because I had walking pneumonia and a double ear infection. On top of that, he'd also prescribed a sleep aid in light of the fact that the steroid would likely cause me to have trouble sleeping.

So, yes, three medications and one groggy morning later, I woke up to find my laptop next to me in bed and I thought, *Uh oh.* (I know what you're asking: *Why would you assume the worst about yourself, Lisa?* Because one time I'd used my laptop while on sleep aids and unwittingly signed up for an expensive, yearlong book-of-the-month club with an ironclad contract that forced me to pay $19.99 per month no matter what, and I'd also come dangerously close to buying a time-share in Cabo. Clearly, I wanted to read by the beach.) Then that sinking feeling got even heavier when my fuzzy head cleared up enough to remember the cold, hard truth: I'd tried to email a Dear John message to the potential beau in the middle of my *drowsy-loony* phase the night before.

I immediately opened the dating app and hurriedly scrolled down my *sent* messages—and there it was. In irrefutable, black-and-white digital form was a rambling message that said I was sorry we wouldn't work out romantically but that maybe one day I could come over and . . . wait for it: *sit on his lap*! To this day, I don't know how my brain scrambled *maybe I could meet your cats* with *maybe I could sit on your lap* but it did and, needless to say, that was the mortifying end of online dating for me.

In my admittedly limited but oh-so-humiliating experience, dates just aren't as fulfilling when they're dependent on a Wi-Fi signal. I want real, face-to-face relationships with real intimacy. Thank heaven, Jesus is not some faraway, wannabe suitor using a fancy filter to make Himself look more attractive. Instead, He is the up-close and perfectly passionate Lover of the Bride, His church. He is the Groom who, by giving us His Spirit here and now, offers us infinitely more than a long-distance relationship while we wait to unite with Him once again in glory.

- **IT'S WIDELY UNDERSTOOD** that a soon-to-be bride's priorities are securing a venue, picking out a dress, and choosing her bridesmaids. What do you think our priorities should be as the spiritual soon-to-be bride of Christ?

- **ON A SCALE** of 1 to 10, with 1 being *I can't remember His name* and 10 being *We know what the other one is thinking before we even put it into words*, how would you define the level of intimacy in your love relationship with Jesus?

Day 5

JESUS CARES ABOUT THE
LITTLE THINGS IN OUR LIVES

"Aren't two sparrows sold for a penny? Yet not one of them falls to the ground without your Father's consent. But even the hairs of your head have all been counted. So don't be afraid; you are worth more than many sparrows." MATTHEW 10:29–31

—————————

FOR A PLETHORA OF reasons Missy's transition to middle school was a difficult one. Mind you, she was a positive little trooper through it all. And while we both cried over a couple of situations where her tender heart was unnecessarily poked, I'm the only one who fantasized about walloping the one who wounded her. Sometimes the bear in my mama heart just won't stay down no matter how many proverbial tranquilizer darts I self-inject!

I'm old-school when it comes to toughing it out because my Dad Harper (My dad's first name wasn't "Harper" it was Everett, the reason I refer to him as "Dad Harper" is to distinguish him from my stepfather, Dad Angel!)—who put himself through college busting broncs in weekend rodeos—taught me to always get back on the horse who bucked you off, otherwise fear would begin to own you. Therefore, persevering through hard times is a recurrent theme in our house. One of my favorite pep talks involves the somewhat cheesy if-it-wasn't-for-the-struggle-in-the-cocoon-the-butterfly's-wings-would-never-unfold-and-it-would-never-fly metaphor that poor Missy's heard so many times it's a wonder her eyes don't roll right back in her head when I repeat it! But, after one too many negative incidents at her old school, I became aware that toughing it out was beginning to do serious harm to my daughter's emotional well-being.

After a lot of prayer and consulting with a counselor and other education professionals, I went with my gut and transferred her to a new Christian school. The downside is she enrolled several weeks after the other students began classes, so they already knew the ropes of where each class meets, what the teachers' personalities are like, and what are the most popular games to play during recess. More important, her peers had established friend groups. My precious kid already stands out because she's a beautiful Haitian instead of a born and bred American; her English isn't quite as clear as a kid who was born in the U.S.; she doesn't have the same drawl as indigenous Southerners because she only spoke Creole until I brought her home to Tennessee when she was almost five years old; and I'm a single, adoptive mom who's pushing sixty instead of a perky, Pilates-practicing thirty-something with a husband and a minivan! All of which means: it took Missy quite a while to catch up and make friends.

I know I can't—and shouldn't—protect her from every single inevitable bump on this road called life. I know without the grit there'd be no pearl. That the brightest dawns come after the darkest nights. That the best wine is the result of an elongated crushing process. Blah, blah, blah. But all those truisms pale when you watch your sweet child—who's already endured her first mama's death, soul-crushing abandonment, potentially fatal medical issues, and abuse in a Third World orphanage—begin to hemorrhage hope. It all but ripped my guts out to watch her spirits sag and her confidence wane.

But God.

At her school's recent monthly chapel service (which parents are invited to attend), her gracious principal, Miss Amy, announced they were going to start honoring one male and one female student from each class at every chapel who exemplified an aspect of the character of Jesus Christ. I almost fell out of my chair when she got to the sixth grade and announced: "Missy Harper." I had to bite my lip while watching her walk to the front of the auditorium, grinning shyly the whole way. And a significant amount of water weight rolled down my face while Amy explained how Missy exuded joy in the classroom, in the hallways, at lunchtime, and even in math class.

I know it wasn't the Heisman or an Oscar or a purple heart. To the casual observer, it was just a small nod, in a small school, to a small girl who's taking small steps toward maturity. But to me, it was no small miracle. It was a tangible reminder that our Savior cares about every single detail of our lives. Even those seemingly insignificant moments in our story that appear minuscule to others matter to Him because WE MATTER TO HIM. For those of you who feel missed, marginalized, or like you're standing outside some sort of communal merry-go-round that everyone's riding except you today, may I remind you that you're neither alone nor invisible? Jesus will never miss a beat in your life.

- **IN WHAT CIRCUMSTANCES** do you feel especially unseen and alone?

- **READ MARK 10:13-16** and 12:41–44. What do these passages reveal about how Jesus noticed and cared for people most would've ignored?

Day 6

JESUS IS *THE* KING OF *ALL* KINGS

Then I saw heaven opened, and there was a white horse. Its rider is called Faithful and True, and with justice he judges and makes war. His eyes were like a fiery flame, and many crowns were on his head. He had a name written that no one knows except himself. He wore a robe dipped in blood, and his name is called the Word of God. The armies that were in heaven followed him on white horses, wearing pure white linen. A sharp sword came from his mouth, so that he might strike the nations with it. He will rule them with an iron rod. He will also trample the winepress of the fierce anger of God, the Almighty. And he has a name written on his robe and on his thigh: KING OF KINGS and LORD OF LORDS. REVELATION 19:11–16, EMPHASIS MINE

HAVE YOU EVER THOUGHT you were decent at something till you ran smack-dab into someone totally out of your league? I have. I was a decent high school volleyball player (good enough to earn a volleyball scholarship to college and even get my picture in the local paper!). And by the end of my first collegiate season, I'd progressed from good to better as a result of hundreds of hours in the gym running drills, scrimmaging, and playing tournaments. By my senior year, I'd progressed into a strong volleyball player at the Division 1 AA level and was even recognized as Player of the Week by our local McDonalds, which earned me an extra-large serving of chicken nuggets and fries!

But not long after graduation, my competitive context was significantly widened when I got invited to play in an exhibition game with a couple of other former collegiate volleyball players. For some sadistic reason the coach decided to put me at the net directly across from a very nice, very tall girl who'd been an All-American at the University of Nebraska and had played on the Olympic team.

I don't remember how long it took for the ball to get set to her because I was just desperately trying to mirror her lightning-fast lateral movements in the hopes of blocking the ball she was going to try and slam onto our side of the court. But when it happened, everything came into hyper-focus. I squatted so deep in preparation to block her attack that my fanny almost kissed the court, then I sprang upwards with what felt like the coiled power of a cobra. I jumped so high that both my hands and forearms soared above the net, effectively creating a flesh wall that would surely be impenetrable, even for an Olympian.

Time stood still as I hung there suspended in space, simultaneously watching her left arm whip forward with such power and velocity that the gleaming white Tachikara volleyball exploded through my wimpy "wall" and struck me smack in the face so hard that it knocked me flat on my back. People who witnessed our lopsided encounter at the net described it as a rowboat going head-to-head with the Titanic! Every time I remember that rather humiliating collision on the volleyball court, the children's song—*One of these things is not like the other ones*—begins to play in my head!

When Scripture describes Jesus as *The* King of *all* kings (1 Tim. 6:15; Rev. 17:14; 19:16), it's painting the portrait of One who's different than all other kings, queens, emperors, presidents, prime ministers, chiefs, multi-starred generals, and rulers in human history. And infinitely more unique than the volleyball phenom I faced (who normally competed against world-class athletes like herself, not regular-class chicks like me), Jesus is in a league completely by Himself. He's transcendent; there's never been and never will be a sovereign like our Savior. Which is why people had a hard time wrapping their minds around His reign during His earthly ministry. Even James and John, who were some of those closest to Jesus, assumed He'd ultimately rule over some type of humanish, status-obsessed, power-seeking kingdom as evidenced by how they tried to curry future favor: "When you sit on your glorious throne," they said, "we want to sit in places of honor next to you, one on your right and the other on your left." To which Jesus responded: "You don't know what you are asking! Are you able to drink from the bitter cup of suffering I am about to drink?" (Mark 10: 37–38a NLT).

Geez Louise, they might as well have asked the Messiah to use His omniscience to help them pick numbers for the Power Ball!

It's not until the King of all kings condescends to a criminal's death on a cross that a Roman centurion—who would hardly qualify as religious—recognized the supremacy of Jesus. The title "centurion" indicates that he was an enlisted man who had the guts and gumption to rise through the ranks and become a military leader.[6] This means he'd surely seen his share of deceitful despots and evil emperors, given the greed and violence of the Greco-Roman era. Furthermore, Roman coins during that time were all inscribed: *Tiberius*

Caesar, son of the divine Augustus, so Roman citizens only referred to Caesar as the "Son of God."[7] But watching the crucifixion compelled this tough-as-nails soldier to realize he'd been bowing to the wrong ruler:

> When it was noon, darkness came over the whole land until three in the afternoon. And at three Jesus cried out with a loud voice, *"Eloi, Eloi, lemá sabachtháni?"* which is translated, "My God, my God, why have you abandoned me?" . . . Jesus let out a loud cry and breathed his last. Then the curtain of the temple was torn in two from top to bottom. *When the centurion, who was standing opposite him, saw the way he breathed his last, he said, "Truly this man was the Son of God!"* (Mark 15:33–34, 37–39, emphasis mine)

It wasn't an imperial palace, a gilded throne, or hordes of adoring citizens submitting to His authority that convinced the centurion Jesus was divine; it was His sacrificial death. And since that first Easter weekend, Christianity is the only religion in the world whose belief system centers around a Savior who suffered. We're the only ones who place our hope in a deity who was willing to die so that we could live. Only a king like that—who chose to lay down His crown and be crushed on behalf of His people—can rightfully be called *The King of all* kings.

- **HAS ANYONE EVER** made a significant sacrifice on your behalf (i.e., a parent sacrificing something they needed so that you could have something you needed—like giving up the possibility of a new vehicle so you could get braces or have college tuition)? If so, how did their sacrifice affect your loyalty toward them?

- **READ MARK 10:45.** How would you paraphrase Jesus's "mission statement" to a non-Christian?

- **READ 1 TIMOTHY 6:11–16.** How would you describe the relationship between the supremacy of Jesus and our pursuit of righteousness?

Day 7

JESUS IS THE ONLY TRULY SAFE TIME MACHINE

As they were walking along the road, a man said to him, "I will follow you wherever you go." Jesus replied, "Foxes have dens and birds have nests, but the Son of Man has no place to lay his head. He said to another man, "Follow me." But he replied, "Lord, first <u>let me go</u> and bury my father." Jesus said to him, "Let the dead bury their own dead, but you go and proclaim the kingdom of God." Still another said, "I will follow you, Lord; but first let me <u>go back</u> and say goodbye to my family." Jesus replied, "No one who puts a hand to the plow and <u>looks back</u> is fit for service in the kingdom of God." LUKE 9:57–62 NIV, EMPHASIS MINE

Now Jesus loved Martha and her sister and Lazarus. So when he heard that Lazarus was sick, he stayed where he was two more days, and then he said to his disciples, "Let us <u>go back</u> to Judea." "But Rabbi," they said, "a short while ago the Jews there tried to stone you, and yet you are <u>going back</u>?" . . . [Jesus] went on to tell them, "Our friend Lazarus has fallen asleep; but I am going there to wake him up." JOHN 11:5–8, 11 NIV, EMPHASIS MINE

I RECENTLY HEARD A pastor teach about how honest reflection is healthy but how an ongoing preoccupation with the past or acute nostalgia—longing to go back to a previous time in your life—can be dangerous. Naturally, this got me to thinking about my history, and about the passages I've read in Scripture about "going back" to some former place we've once been. In some places Jesus tells us *not* to go back—to press forward (see Luke 9 above). Yet in other places (see John 11 above), He shepherds His followers to do the opposite, to go back, even at great risk. And, over time, I've come to realize the difference between the two.

Forty years ago I was a sophomore in college, besotted with all things preppy, anxious about who to invite to the Kappa Delta winter formal, and trying to earn the approval of everyone I met. Yet while I masqueraded as a happy-go-lucky, Christian sorority girl, I was convinced that God was disappointed with me. Because while I'd been raised by a Jesus-loving mama who didn't play when it came to being in church every time the doors were open, praying before every meal, reading the Bible every morning and evening, and who strongly encouraged me to fork over a big chunk of my lifeguarding money to the Lottie Moon offering, I was also carrying heavy shame that came with the sense of abandonment caused when my dad left us to quickly marry the "other woman," as well as the sexual molestation and abuse I experienced multiple times throughout childhood and adolescence. Even as I was leading Bible studies with a big, chatty crew of other coeds, I secretly wondered how in the world a perfect God could completely accept and unconditionally love a damaged girl like me.

If I could give my nineteen-year-old-running-scared-and-pretending-to-have-it-all-together self some advice, it would be these three basic truths:

1. Jesus's love isn't based on our deservedness or lack thereof; it's rooted in His character, not ours.

2. The Bible's overarching story proves that our Savior has a soft spot for the precious people our world cruelly dismisses as losers; in fact, most of the people He elevates as leaders for kingdom causes came from the scratch-and-dent bin!

3. There's no dark side to our Creator Redeemer. If you've put your faith in Jesus and the biblical truth that He's already justified us by His sacrificial death on a cross and subsequent bodily resurrection, you can exhale and lean fully into His embrace because, though this life will come with ups and downs, no other proverbial shoe is going to drop when it comes to your eternal future.

It's taken decades of time spent with Jesus and time spent in a Christian therapist's office for me to sort through the emotional detritus in my history and separate past memories into "keep" and "discard" bins. It took lots of hard work, buckets of tears, and consistent and safe counseling to learn to *feel* what our Great Physician would ultimately *heal*. Mind you, I'm not "fixed"—my heart still bears a few jagged scars—but I'm freer than I ever hoped to be.

History doesn't have an unhealthy grip on my heart and mind anymore. In fact, now I can see clearly how Jesus was/is compassionately attuned and accessible to me in every, single moment of my life, even during the super sad or scary times. The last piece of advice I've learned to remind my almost-sixty-year-old self of is this: don't take field trips to the sinkholes of the past unless He's driving the bus!

Why do I say that? Because in Luke 9, the people who wanted to "go back" were doing so without Jesus—and for motivations He could discern weren't quite up to snuff. (In those times, funeral events happened twice; the first one being for mourning and proper burial, and the second being about receiving inheritance. Upon rigorous study, scholars say the people who wanted to "go back" in Luke 9 were preoccupied with obtaining family money, and Jesus wanted their allegiance to be with Him, not finances.) But in John 11, Jesus Himself ushered His own disciples to "go back" to Judea, even at great risk to the whole group, for the sake of resurrecting the dead. When *Jesus* is truly the one leading you to go back, follow Him! He is probably up to regenerating old, dead parts of you that need new life!

- **WHAT CHAPTER(S) OF** your life—if any—would you like to completely obliterate from memory?

- **IF YOU HAVEN'T** already, are you willing to revisit that season with Jesus as your wise guide and perfectly protective guard?

Day 8

JESUS IS A MESSIAH TO EVERY ETHNICITY

When Jesus learned that the Pharisees had heard he was making and baptizing more disciples than John (though Jesus himself was not baptizing, but his disciples were), he left Judea and went again to Galilee. <u>He had to travel through Samaria</u>; so he came to a town of Samaria called Sychar near the property that Jacob had given his son Joseph. Jacob's well was there, and Jesus, worn out from his journey, sat down at the well. It was about noon. JOHN 4:1–6, EMPHASIS MINE

WHEN I FIRST BROUGHT Missy home from Haiti, I was so gratefully discombobulated that God miraculously chose me to be her second, adoptive mom, it was all I could do not to dress us in matching outfits! And while I was in that honeymoon stage of brand-new motherhood (frankly, I'm still pretty much in the honeymoon stage and our adoption was finalized nine years ago!), I subconsciously assumed others recognized this tiny, big-brown-eyed daughter of mine as a tangible kiss from God too. I can still remember one afternoon, not too long after Missy came home, when we were walking hand-in-hand down the sidewalk of Main Street in Franklin, Tennessee, which is a small, postcard-worthy Southern town near our home. I noticed an elderly gentleman who was walking toward us and seemed to be looking at us with a big grin on his face. I squeezed Missy's hand, straightened my shoulders, put a little more pep in my step, and smiled back at him, thinking: *Yep, somehow that man knows this kid right here is a flat-out miracle, baby!*

Unfortunately, my visual acuity is decreasing as my age increases and I wasn't wearing glasses that day; as the gap between us narrowed, I realized he wasn't grinning—he was grimacing. Then, as he was passing by, he glared at me for a long moment, hissed in a low, menacing voice, "That's disgusting," and spit right in front of our feet. Evidently, that grumpy old man was so blinded by the fact that Missy is a beautiful Haitian child and I'm a middle-aged pale lady that he missed the miracle. Sometimes I forget that we live less than an hour from where the Ku Klux Klan was founded in 1865 and there are still folks who are vehemently opposed to multi-ethnic families. Sadly, his heart was so shriveled by racism that he couldn't appreciate how God had healed this precious little girl whom doctors in Port-au-Prince predicted wouldn't live to see her third birthday, and had restored unto me decades that had been devoured by locusts when He allowed me to become a late-in-life parent.

For as long as I can remember, I've resonated with outliers and outcasts like the Samaritans in the Bible, but it wasn't until I had the undeserved blessing of becoming Missy's second mom that I realized they're part of my spiritual family tree—although my ancient ancestors had to deal with much more painful prejudice than a little spittle from a spiteful octogenarian.

In order to understand the bigotry Samaritans faced and the reason for the rift between them and their Jewish neighbors, you have to go all the way back to the 900s BC and the reign of King Solomon, who was the third king of Israel and who was also an ancient "player" with hundreds of foreign wives who competed fiercely with each other for his heart and his wallet. Therefore, most of his kids weren't what you'd call close siblings. So, when Solomon died, the baton pass to a clear heir was bungled, and his son Rehoboam was such a horrible leader that the nation of Israel ended up splitting into two kingdoms: the Southern Kingdom (also called Judah, which retained the crown jewel of Jerusalem) and the Northern Kingdom (which retained the name Israel). Two hundred years later, in 721 BC, the Northern Kingdom of Israel fell to a warring people group called the Assyrians. Most of the people of Israel were led off to Assyria as captives, but some remained in the land and intermarried with foreigners planted there by the Assyrians. Some scholars say that was Assyria's way of further subjugating the Jews by diluting their bloodlines, and this half-Jewish, half-Gentile people group became known as the Samaritans.

The first time Samaritans appear in the Bible's narrative is the books of Ezra and Nehemiah (400s BC), when the Israelites returned to Jerusalem from the Babylonian captivity and were called to rebuild the walls around Jerusalem. The Samaritans, who'd moved into the area while the Israelites were in captivity, opposed the renewal project and tried to sabotage Nehemiah's rebuilding efforts. However, Nehemiah was not a contractor to be trifled with (Neh. 6:8–9)! This turf war began a centuries-long feud between Jews and Samaritans—the Samaritans now known not only as half-breeds, but as traitors, too.

The Samaritans went on to establish their own temple on Mount Gerizim (which the woman at the well talks about later in John 4) and only adhered to Torah—the first five books of the Old Testament—instead of all the Hebrew Scriptures. They also declared the Jewish priesthood illegitimate and established their own version. Between their familial alliances with Assyrians, forsaking the rebuilding of Jerusalem's wall, cherry-picking the Hebrew Bible, and instituting their own leaders instead of following the rules appointed in the Law, the bottom line is that the Samaritans desecrated everything an Orthodox Jew held sacred. By the time of Jesus's earthly ministry, Jewish resentment toward Samaritans ran so deep that they publicly cursed them in synagogues and prayed for Jehovah to exclude them from eternal life.

With that context in mind, it becomes clear that when John 4 portrays Jesus as *having to* pass through Samaria, it isn't a random geographical footnote. In fact, this seemingly innocuous detail probably provoked some of his first-century audience the way the sight of Missy and I holding hands and all but skipping down the sidewalk of a small, Southern town provoked that hateful, old saliva-slinger. Because when John described our Creator-Redeemer as *having to* enter a territory that Orthodox Jews would have scrupulously avoided even if it meant traveling many miles out of the way, He was underscoring the culture-challenging, prejudice-pummeling, implausibly inclusive grace of our Savior. Don't forget, as the second person of the Trinity, Jesus is perfectly omniscient—all-knowing. Which means He knew exactly who He'd encounter at the well during the scorching heat of that particular Middle Eastern day. He was more than familiar with every excruciating detail of how that Samaritan woman had been kicked to the curb by five husbands, as well as being ostracized by the "upstanding" members of ancient society. He was compelled to go to Samaria because He is the Great Physician and broken hearts are His specialty, no matter what lovely hue of skin envelops it. To both Jew and Gentile, Hebrew or Samaritan—or any ethnicity in the world today—He offers himself as Messiah for all who believe, and He can heal *anyone's* past, self-righteous prude and traitor alike!

- **READ REVELATION 21:1-4 (NIV).** In the Greek language this passage was originally penned in, the word *people* in verse 3 is actually "peoples" (some Bible translations still render it singular), and it illustrates that people groups will still maintain their nationality/ethnicity in heaven! Why do you think some people of faith still practice racial prejudice when the story of Scripture reveals it's not remotely biblically defensible?

- **DO YOU HAVE** a lot of friends who don't look like you, talk like you, or think like you? On a scale of 1 to 10, with 1 being *nervous as a cat* and 10 being *grateful and content*, how comfortable are you worshipping in a racially diverse church?

Day 9

JESUS IS PERFECTLY COMPLETE
AND SELF-FULFILLED

I do not call you servants anymore, because a servant doesn't know what his master is doing. I have called you friends, because I have made known to you everything I have heard from my Father. JOHN 15:15

———————————

I KNOW I TOOK a big literary risk to weave entries about the incarnate nature of Jesus Christ at the beginning of this pretty devotional instead of waiting until I'd hopefully whetted your reading appetite with lighter, more humorous fare. It was not unlike taking a first date home to meet your parents and then awkwardly wedging together on the sagging living room sofa to peruse family photo albums! I can all but hear a few of you sighing inwardly quite loudly. So we're going to take a dance break to shake off any reading cobwebs that may have accumulated. Well, almost anyway.

In the eighth century, church father and theologian John of Damascus began using the Greek word *perichoresis*, which means "going around, rotation," to describe the ongoing union within the Godhead. And one of the root words of choreography is *choreia*, which is a very close cousin of *choresis*, so it's not too much of an etymological stretch to describe the Trinity as an ongoing, circular dance! Pretty cool, huh?

Okay, my gut says that despite that nifty *Dancing with the Supernatural Stars* illustration, a few of you are still scratching your heads, musing: "Alright, I get why the Trinity was important back in the day when the church really needed clear terms for who Jesus was, but now that we've figured that out, why in the world should it matter to us today?" Which brings me to another one of my super-smart imaginary boyfriends, St. Augustine, who put it this way: "Only the Christian God is a perfect community unto Himself."

In other words, God didn't create us because He was lonely nor is Jesus inclined toward us because He doesn't have any other friends! There's a lovely dissonance between being needed and being wanted, y'all. Because being needed puts the onus squarely on us—on our continued performance, ability, and usefulness. But being wanted puts the onus on God, on His sovereign choice to redeem us through the death and resurrection of Jesus and then adopt us into His forever family when we put our hope and belief in what He sacrificed and accomplished on our behalf.

No doubt you've heard—or seen splashed across social media—phraseology that goes something like this: *There is a God-shaped hole in the heart of every human that can only be satisfied by God Himself.* (That catchy spiritual concept, by the way, is based on an ancient publication entitled *Pensées* by a French mathematician, philosopher, and theologian named Blaise Pascal.) And while I deeply resonate with and agree with Pascal's premise, I think it's important for us to clarify that the reverse isn't true. *Our Creator Redeemer doesn't have a human-shaped hole in His heart.* He doesn't *need* mankind to be fulfilled or satisfied. Which may sound callous at first, but if you'll ponder the truism of God's self-fulfillment for a moment or two, I think you'll begin to see the miraculous implication of Jesus's incarnation. The Son of God is transcendent—a perfectly preexisting, omniscient, and self-fulfilled person of the Godhead, perfectly "above" and "other" from all that He has created. Yet He *chose* to be immanent (to be knowable or graspable to us). He *chose* to not just come near, but *enter*, His creation. He *chose* to be close to us and commune with us for His good pleasure! He didn't have to. He didn't need to. He *wanted* to.

On the days it feels like you need to work hard enough to make Jesus happy, remember: He was happy in His Trinitarian existence well before He ever created the world. He had all the community and fulfillment a person could dream of. And yet He decided to create a world, and more than that, to enter that world by putting on flesh to save that world—to save *you*—all because *it delighted Him to do so.*

If that doesn't make your heart sing, you might need an EKG, honey.

- **READ GENESIS 1:26–27,** 2 Corinthians 13:13, and Galatians 4:4–6. What common denominator do you find in all three passages?

- **HOW WOULD YOU** explain the significance of Jesus choosing to be with us to someone who thinks they have to "earn" His affection with good behavior?

- **HOW WOULD YOU** explain to a friend that it's *really good news for us* that, as the second person of the Trinity, Jesus is totally satisfied and happy within the Godhead?

Day 10

JESUS IS A TRUTH-TELLER

*He came to Nazareth, where he had been brought up. As usual, he entered the synagogue on the Sabbath day and stood up to read. The scroll of the prophet Isaiah was given to him, and unrolling the scroll, he found the place where it **was** written:*

*The Spirit of the Lord is on me, because he has anointed me
to preach good news to the poor. He has sent me
to proclaim release to the captives and recovery of sight to the blind,
to set free the oppressed, to proclaim the year of the Lord's favor.*

He then rolled up the scroll, gave it back to the attendant, and sat down. And the eyes of everyone in the synagogue were fixed on him. He began by saying to them, "<u>Today as you listen, this Scripture has been fulfilled</u>." They were all speaking well of him and were amazed by the gracious words that came from his mouth; yet they said, "Isn't this Joseph's son?" LUKE 4:16–22, EMPHASIS MINE

WHEN JESUS BEGAN PREACHING to His friends and family in Nazareth, that home crowd was initially supportive. They were probably packed into that little synagogue like sardines, curiously anticipating what Joe and Mary's firstborn had to say. Archeologists estimate the population of Nazareth was less than five hundred people during the time of Christ,[8] so surely most everyone in the crowd that day had known Jesus since He was a tiny tyke. They'd watched Him grow up and become an apprentice with His adoptive dad. Many had attended His going away party the week before He set off to become a traveling rabbi. Several nudged each other and nodded when He began to read from the scroll of Isaiah, thinking, *He must do a lot of public speaking on the road because He's gotten so eloquent. We should invite Him back to teach more often!*

One of my favorite Gospel commentators, William Hendriksen, describes the scene like this:

> The atmosphere in the probably crowded synagogue is surcharged with curiosity. Everybody in the audience is wondering what their townsman, the former carpenter, about whom they have been hearing so much of late, is going to say in elucidation and application of the Scripture passage he has read a moment ago . . .

All is quiet, so quiet that one can hear a feather drop. Every eye is fixated on Jesus. He opens His mouth. He begins his address. Does he start out by reminding the audience of the golden days, now gone forever, when Jehovah stretched out his mighty arm and performed miracles on the earth? He does not. Does he begin by entertaining his listeners with bright promises pertaining to the future? Not that either.[9]

Right when Jesus had the audience in the palm of His hand, He proclaimed something that was less popular than a WeightWatchers speaker at a Krispy Kreme conference:

"These Scriptures came true today!" (Luke 4:21b TLB)

In other words, "I'm the fulfillment of Isaiah's Messianic prophecy—I'm the Living Hope you've spent centuries praying for!"

And when it dawned on His friends and neighbors that Joe and Mary's boy whom they'd known from the time He was in Pampers wasn't just talking *about* God, He was declaring to *be* God, they were livid:

These remarks stung them to fury; and jumping up, they mobbed him and took him to the edge of the hill on which the city was built, to push him over the cliff. But he walked away through the crowd and left them. (Luke 4:28–30 TLB)

It's one thing for strangers or rivals to attempt to push you off a cliff, but it's a whole other deal when you went to elementary school with the guys doing the shoving. Truth is transformative; it will flat out set you free. But it can also get you in trouble with the folks who've grown comfortable with their own ingrained, unbudging expectations about who you are. None of us is divine, of course, but may we all take our cues from Jesus and tell the truth, no matter what our listeners might assume about us.

- **WOULD YOUR CLOSEST** friends and family describe you as a straight-forward, "just the facts" kind of communicator or as someone who "seasons" or "softens" hard truths to make them less offensive?

- **READ NUMBERS 23:19** and Colossians 4:6. How would you explain the synergy between always telling the truth and yet seasoning it with grace to a child or new Christian?

Day 11

JESUS IS COMFORTABLE
BEING UNCOMFORTABLE

When Jesus saw a large crowd around him, he gave the order to go to the other side of the sea. A scribe approached him and said, "Teacher, I will follow you wherever you go." Jesus told him, "Foxes have dens, and birds of the sky have nests, but the Son of Man has no place to lay his head." MATTHEW 8:18–20

MY DAD WAS LIKE John Wayne in miniature, and when I was a little girl, I wanted to be just like him. When I found out he rode bulls in the rodeo to help put himself through college, I was determined to do the same thing and secretly began training by leaping on our very docile and unsuspecting milk cows on the far side of the pasture out of Dad's sight. But the first time I tried to pounce on one of our bulls, I ended up with a very bruised behind. When Dad noticed my limp and made me spill the beans about how I'd gotten hurt, he was quiet for a minute or two. Then he put it plainly: "Lisa, if you want to be a champion bull-rider, you're going to need a harder heinie."

I have no idea how tough their posteriors were, but there was a group of ancient Christ-followers in the 1400s called stylites or "pillar saints" (based on the Greek word *stylos*, which means "pillar" or "column"), who certainly had tough *feet*! They followed the extreme and ascetic practice of moving away from civilization into the wilderness and making their "home" atop pillars that had been dragged there for that sole purpose, so as to avoid distractions and devote themselves entirely to God. This incredibly uncomfortable practice was initiated in 423 BC by Simeon the Elder and continued until the mid-1400s. One saint named Alypius is recorded as standing upright on a column less than four feet in diameter for fifty-three years until his ankles collapsed. However, instead of descending from his pillar and going to a podiatrist, he laid down on his side and spent the last fourteen years of his life prone on that airy altar!

Now quite frankly, I think the pillar saints' "statuesque" acts of faith, while well-intentioned, are a bit bonkers. I've been studying the Bible for almost forty years and have yet to find a single verse that advocates hanging out alone on a glorified column to please God. However, as bizarre as their devotion appears in the context of our modern, comfort-obsessed culture, I find myself admiring their radical willingness to kick ease to the curb for the sake of Christ.

And remember, comfort wasn't high on the agenda of our Messiah either. He didn't begin His ministry with a parade, where He was lauded a populist hero while riding in some cushy carriage. Instead, His everlasting reign as the King of all kings commenced in the obscurity of the wilderness, where He fasted from food for forty days and still perfectly resisted satan's temptations. Then the Prince of Peace spent the next three years of His public ministry as an outlier, shunned even in places you would've thought He'd be celebrated (like the hometown He grew up in [Luke 4:16–30]). And while His divine purpose was beyond difficult and utterly depleting, He didn't fly first class or stay in nice hotels to recoup, but was effectively homeless with *no place to lay His head.*

Furthermore, our Savior wasn't simply a mortgage-less sojourner who had to crash on friends' couches or camp out in the fields. He was also betrayed by those closest to Him. His mom and dad literally forgot Him at the temple when He was just a kid. His neighbors tried to kill Him. And one of His closest friends threw Him under the bus at His greatest point of need, just prior to His murder on the cross.

Based on all the Bible tells us about His experience on this earth, it's probably not too much of a stretch to describe Jesus as rarely comfortable or comforted. Which makes sense in light of His self-proclaimed mission statement:

> Jesus called them over and said to them, "You know that those who are regarded as rulers of the Gentiles lord it over them, and those in high positions act as tyrants over them. But it is not so among you. On the contrary, whoever wants to become great among you will be your servant, and whoever wants to be first among you will be a slave to all. *For even the Son of Man did not come to be served, but to serve, and to give his life as a ransom for many."* (Mark 10:42–45, emphasis mine)

If we want to live more *Christophormic* lives—which just means lives that are shaped like Jesus—we'd better learn how to get comfortable with being uncomfortable.

- **WHICH IS EASIER** for you to give up: physical comfort (like air-conditioning or nice furnishings) or emotional comfort (like support, encouragement, and/or approval from other people)? Why?

- **READ MATTHEW 16:24-26.** What constitutes a figurative "cross" you've chosen to pick up and carry in order to closely follow Jesus?

- **IF YOUR WALK** with God has been mostly comfortable and easy lately, how might Jesus's example challenge you toward change? What might He be asking you to sacrifice in this season that perhaps you've been putting off?

Day 12

JESUS IS LORD OF THE SABBATH

Jesus entered the synagogue again, and a man was there who had a shriveled hand. In order to accuse him, they were watching him closely to see whether he would heal him on the Sabbath. He told the man with the shriveled hand, "Stand before us." Then he said to them, "Is it lawful to do good on the Sabbath or to do evil, to save life or to kill?" But they were silent. After looking around at them with anger, he was grieved at the hardness of their hearts and told the man, "Stretch out your hand." So he stretched it out, and his hand was restored. Immediately the Pharisees went out and started plotting with the Herodians against him, how they might kill him. MARK 3:1–6

THE FIRST IMAGES THAT used to race forward in my mind when I heard the word *Sabbath* were of prudish bathing suits and push mowers. Because when I was growing up, our mom was emphatic about keeping the Sabbath (which Scripture basically defines as a day of abstaining from secular work that follows each six-day working week[10]) *holy.* And for a Southern-Baptist-to-the-bone woman like my mama, the Sabbath definitely meant Sunday, not the twenty-four-hour time period from sundown on Friday night through sundown on Saturday night like those who follow a more Judaic or literal Old Testament tradition. In my mama's world, *holy* meant not only did I have to use my inside voice while clad in a prissy dress and uncomfortable shoes for the better part of the day we spent at church, it also meant I couldn't swim in a two-piece bathing suit when we got home. Thankfully, our pool was in the backyard surrounded by a privacy fence so at least she allowed us to swim on hot Sunday afternoons, but my sister and I had to wear one-piece bathing suits because I guess belly buttons are bad news on *The Lord's Day* (a phrase I repeated as a child with hushed reverence and apprehension because I'd rebelled a few times when mom left home to visit relatives on Sunday afternoons and sneakily wore my verboten bikini in her absence, so I half-expected to be zapped by divine lightning at any given moment).

Based on my dear, well-intentioned mom's understanding of what Christians *couldn't* do on Sunday (no belly button bearing, no loud talking, no loud music, no lawn mowing, no freeze tag playing, no bike riding, no TV watching, no

Burger King loitering with friends), by the time I could read I'd deduced that God was a grumpy disciplinarian, determined to make His kids well-behaved rule-followers, even if it meant squashing their joy once a week.

Therefore, it's been such a sweet relief to discover our heavenly Father instituted a day of rest every week as a *loving parameter* not a *legalistic principle.* Remember when our heavenly Father initially enforced a guideline regarding Sabbath (Exod. 16:27–30), the Israelites had just followed Moses out of Egypt after *four hundred years in captivity.*

They were as wobbly as newborn calves when it came to this whole liberation thing because they had no experience or understanding of what freedom felt like. For as long as their grandparents and great-grandparents and great-great-grandparents could remember, they'd existed as slaves under the mostly cruel ownership of their archenemies, the Egyptians. A Jewish slave's sole purpose in Egyptian culture during that era was to do the brutal, backbreaking work of mixing mud and straw to make bricks and hauling heavy stones in the oppressive Middle Eastern heat. Based on historical accounts from that ancient era, their hands were likely covered in thick callouses and many of their backs were covered in scars from regular beatings.[11] And they existed like that for so long they rarely even daydreamed about liberty anymore.

But God!

He met Moses through a flaming topiary and set in motion an audacious plan to rescue His people. I can only imagine how shell-shocked those Hebrews were by the time they set up camp at the base of Mount Sinai after watching the Egyptian army—who was in hot pursuit of them—get swallowed up by the Red Sea! Their entire lives had been spent as captives and now, suddenly, their chains were gone, manna was raining down like doughnuts from heaven, and Yahweh was hovering over them like a protective parent.

With all that in mind, now consider the kindness in this "command":

> "Work six days. The seventh day is a Sabbath, a day of total and complete rest, a sacred assembly. Don't do any work. Wherever you live, it is a Sabbath to GOD." (Lev. 23:3 MSG)

In other words: *You matter so much to Me that I'm not willing to allow you to work your fingers to the bone any longer! Therefore, I've established a twenty-four-hour, no-labor time period so that you can relax and be refueled by leaning into My presence. I want you to sleep late and have the luxury of sitting at the dining table with your family and lingering over a great meal and laughing at your children's jokes. You are My beloved and every single moment of your life exists under the canopy of My grace—but you need to take regular breaks from your busyness to focus on Me and My gifts for you in order to remember that.*

Which was pretty much Jesus's point when He proclaimed: "*The Sabbath was made for man and not man for the Sabbath*" (Mark 2:27, emphasis mine) after some uppity killjoys masquerading as spiritual leaders made a fuss about His disciples harvesting a little grain on the Lord's Day because they were hungry. Over and over again (see Luke 13:10–17; 14:1–6; John 5:1–18; 9:1–41), our Redeemer pushed back against those who tried to twist God's Word into a tool through which they could condemn, shame, or subjugate others.

The Bible was never intended to be used as a club. If we make the mistake of reading it as a rule book, we'll whack the joy and peace out of ourselves and others real quick.

- **DO YOU TEND** to think of "Sabbath" as more of a regulation or a reprieve?

- **HAS THERE BEEN** any inherited theology you've had to unlearn (or may still be considering *unlearning*!) with regard to celebrating a practical Sabbath? If so, what did the Holy Spirit help you understand about resting that was more redemptive?

Day 13
JESUS IS ACCESSIBLY AFFECTIONATE

His disciples stared at one another, at a loss to know which of them he meant. <u>One of them, the disciple whom Jesus loved, was reclining next to him.</u> Simon Peter motioned to this disciple and said, "Ask him which one he means." <u>Leaning back against Jesus</u>, he asked him, "Lord, who is it?" JOHN 13:22–25 NIV, EMPHASIS MINE

Peter turned and saw that the disciple whom Jesus loved was following them. <u>(This was the one who had leaned back against Jesus at the supper and had said, "Lord, who is going to betray you?")</u> JOHN 21:20 NIV, EMPHASIS MINE

———

IN 1944, A MEDICAL experiment was conducted at a research hospital on forty newborn infants to determine whether individuals could thrive alone on basic physiological needs without affection.[12] Twenty newborn infants were housed in a special facility where they had caregivers who would go in to feed them, bathe them, and change their diapers, but they would do nothing else. The caregivers had been instructed not to look at or touch the babies more than what was necessary, never communicating with them. All their physical needs were attended to scrupulously and the environment was kept sterile, none of the babies becoming ill.

The experiment was halted after four months, by which time, at least half of the babies had died at that point. At least two more died even after being rescued and brought into a more natural familial environment. There was no physiological cause for the babies' deaths; they were all physically very healthy. However, before each baby died, there was a period where they would stop verbalizing and trying to engage with their caregivers; generally stop moving, crying, or even changing expression, and death would follow shortly. The babies who had "given up" before being rescued died in the same manner, even though they had been removed from the experimental conditions.

The conclusion of this callous experiment was that physical touch is absolutely vital for humans. Whether we're cognizant of it or not, we all *need* physical connection and the emotional experience of being embraced by another.

Of course, some people will argue that to hope for God to "hold us" is a foolish notion because it ascribes human traits to a divine being, or because it's too emotive. But I beg to differ because the Gospels are crammed full of examples where Jesus touched people with affection and embraced His friends and followers. As a matter of fact, in John 13 we read about John the Beloved (who refers to himself as "the one Jesus loved" five times in his Gospel account) leaning back against Jesus at the Last Supper when he was just a teenager. As a matter a fact, according to Jewish tradition, it was his youth which allowed him to quiz Jesus in the first place because ceremony dictated that the youngest person present at the Passover meal asks the questions. Then at the end of John's Gospel in chapter 21, in the very place where an author typically listed his credentials to prove the legitimacy of the text, John avoids his credentials and instead describes himself as the one who leaned against Jesus. Most scholars think John wrote his Gospel account in his latter years, when he was in his sixties. Which means that this physical embrace with Jesus, which happened approximately FORTY YEARS earlier, is what defined him!

Unfortunately, unlike John the Beloved, far too many of us now emulate the posture of most folks in Jerusalem back then, whom Jesus described as *hesitant to being held*:

> "Jerusalem, Jerusalem, who kills the prophets and stones those who are sent to her. How often I wanted to gather your children together, as a hen gathers her chicks under her wings, *but you were not willing*!" (Luke 13:34, emphasis mine)

We were created to be *held by God*; instead, we settle for a brief pat on the back from a coworker or a wave from another driver in the car pool line.

We were created to be *heard by God*; instead, we settle for a few likes on social media.

We were created to be *healed by God*; instead, we settle by medicating ourselves with busyness, alcohol, fast food, or binge-watching our favorite show.

I wonder how many times a day Jesus affectionately leans toward me, yet I foolishly arch away into distracted isolation. How about you?

- **WITH REGARD TO** your relationship with Jesus, would you describe yourself as more independent and "hesitant to being held" or more like the apostle John, who leaned fully into Jesus's embrace?

- **WHEN IS THE** last time you felt held by Jesus?

Day 14

JESUS DRAWS NEAR TO
THOSE WHO ARE ALIENATED

He also told this parable to some who trusted in themselves that they were righteous and looked down on everyone else: "Two men went up to the temple to pray, one a Pharisee and the other a tax collector. The Pharisee was standing and praying like this about himself: 'God, I thank you that I'm not like other people—greedy, unrighteous, adulterers, or even like this tax collector. I fast twice a week; I give a tenth of everything I get.'

"But the tax collector, standing far off, would not even raise his eyes to heaven but kept striking his chest and saying, 'God, have mercy on me, a sinner!' I tell you, this one went down to his house justified rather than the other, because everyone who exalts himself will be humbled, but the one who humbles himself will be exalted." LUKE 18:9–14

WHEN I WAS AS kid, I loved climbing on the jungle gym in our backyard. It was a twelve-or-so-foot high, hollow-metal-tube apparatus shaped like a pyramid. I haven't seen one like it in a long time—likely because they were the defendant in one too many lawsuits because they got slick from dew in the morning, or after a rain, and got hot enough to burn your hands in the summer, so falls and burns were inevitable. I had the wind knocked out of me multiple times from falling and sustained quite a few blisters myself on that rickety contraption! But by far the worst injury I sustained while scaling that primitive playground equipment was a broken heart.

It was late one afternoon and my best friend at the time (a five-year-old little girl who lived in the house behind us) and I were pretending the jungle gym was our castle. As make-believe princesses in an imaginary tower, we were cooing entreaties down to our invisible princes, when suddenly our soliloquies were interrupted by her mother hollering for her to come down immediately. Sally (name changed to protect the innocent) scrambled down from our perch and sheepishly walked over to her mom.

Sally's mom was a large, loud woman who intimidated me a lot. Frankly, I think she rattled most of the adults in our neighborhood too because her typical tone was just short of a yell, she stomped when she walked, and she almost always wore too-tight, garishly bright, polyester, knee-length shorts. Trust me, when she came barreling toward you, it felt like being stuck in cement shoes in the middle of the highway in front of a speeding, neon SUV!

Which is why when she bellowed for Sally to climb down and meet her at the fence that separated our backyard from theirs, I tried to make myself as small and quiet as possible in order to stay out of her blast zone. Unfortunately, her voice was as booming as her Bermudas, so I clearly heard every word she said. And what came through her clenched teeth is still vivid all these years later: "Sally, I want you to come home this minute! Mr. and Mrs. Harper are getting divorced, so you can't play with Lisa anymore because she's nothing but *trash!*"

I can still remember how my friend glanced apologetically over her shoulder as her mom was pulling her away, and my guess is my face got red-hot with embarrassment. I was ashamed throughout childhood to be regarded by some as inferior because in the 1960s and '70s I was one of only a handful of kids who came from a "broken home" in our small town.

During the earthly ministry of Jesus Christ, Jewish tax collectors were regarded as inferior too, which is apparent by the way they were often lumped in with "sinners" in parables. Although the reason they were scorned didn't have anything to do with the demise of a marriage. Instead, tax collectors—who were also called "publicans" because they collected public revenue on behalf of the government—were infamous for charging whatever the market would bear and then skimming off the top before turning the coffers over to the Roman government, who cruelly imposed heavy tariffs on Israel during the first century. Which meant the tax collectors we often read about in the four Gospel accounts basically bought their Mercedes and fancy Mediterranean homes at the expense of their hardworking neighbors.

However, instead of deriding these unethical embezzlers like most people would have in the Ancient Near East, our Messiah befriended them (remember the short-statured dude name Zacchaeus who climbed up in a sycamore tree?), made one the hero in a widely circulated tale about humility, and intentionally chose one named Matthew to join His team of disciples! King Jesus is the only One who's ever walked this earth who was truly superior to anyone else He rubbed shoulders with, yet He never played that card in a cruel way. He didn't make fun of teammates who struck out in T-ball. He didn't mock schoolmates with noticeable lisps. And He sure didn't snub forlorn pals whose parents were splitting up. When the rest of the world distances themselves from those they consider beneath them using judgmental gestures and voices (and sometimes scary shorts), Jesus mercifully chooses to draw near to those who are alienated. Hallelujah, what a Savior!

- **READ LUKE 19:1-10.** What fresh detail can you find in this true story often dismissed as children's fiction? What does it imply about the inclusive and invitational nature of Jesus?

- **WHO WOULD QUALIFY** as a modern-day "tax collector"—someone who tends to be snubbed or scorned by others—in your circle of friends, acquaintances, or coworkers? What are some practical ways you might be able to align with them instead of avoiding them or alienating them?

Chapter 15

JESUS IS ALWAYS INTERCEDING
ON OUR BEHALF

But because he remains forever, he holds his priesthood permanently. Therefore, he is able to save completely those who come to God through him, <u>since he always lives to intercede for them.</u> HEBREWS 7:24–25, EMPHASIS MINE

Knock, knock.
Who's there?
Interrupting cow.
Interrupting cow, who?
Mooooooooooo!

THAT WAS MISSY'S FAVORITE joke when she was four years old and first learning English. She'd usually erupt into giggles before she even got to the *moo* part, which then gave her the cutest kind of carte blanche to go back to the beginning and start the joke all over again. Of course, by the third or fourth round of knock-knock, we'd both be so tickled it didn't matter whether she got to the end or not! Simply watching Missy's brown eyes twinkle when she said, "Hey Mama, knock, knock!" and listening to her lovely Creole accent when she did her best to pronounce "interrupting" was enough to make my heart swell with affection. In light of everything my little girl had to endure and overcome after her first mom died when she was a baby, just seeing her *alive* is enough for me. But whenever my kid excels at something like doing cannonballs into the pool or multiplying fractions, well, you'd better shut the front door, baby, because this mama will absolutely commence happy dancing—preferably holding a huge, neon sign that says: "THAT'S MY GIRL!"

And the support doesn't stop in the moments she *doesn't* excel at something, either. Even in her hardest moments, her failures, her deepest struggles, I can still be found cheering myself hoarse for her. I'm still 100 percent *for her*. I'm still there to pray with her and advocate for her and ask God for things on her behalf that will help her get back up and take the next step forward.

I've been a Christ-follower since I was itty-bitty, and now I'm oldy-goldy, which means I've known Jesus for more than half a century. Plus, I grew up in a very conservative family and church culture and have been in vocational ministry for more than thirty years. I'm pretty sure I've been exposed to all the Bible stories in some setting or another—Sunday school, Vacation Bible School, Christian summer camp, youth group, worship services, seminary, revivals, women's conferences, small group Bible studies, large group Bible studies, etc. But it wasn't until I experienced what felt like a seismic shift in my heart several years ago when I began a doctoral candidacy at Denver Seminary that I began to actually imagine our holy trinitarian Creator-Redeemer feeling about me the way I feel about my daughter—belly-laughing alongside me, thoroughly delighted that I'm His daughter, pleased as punch that I'm learning new things about Him, and in my corner to help me along no matter what.

Our Savior is *for us*, y'all. He's not gossiping with God the Father about how much weight we gained during COVID. He's not holding a grudge about those Sundays we slept in instead of going to church because we were worn slap out. He's not disappointed that we haven't memorized entire books of the Bible like we were planning to after hearing a super inspirational speaker talk about the importance of Scripture memory at a retreat a few years ago. He's not our adversary; He's our *advocate*! And He doesn't take time off either. Jesus is *interceding* for us (which means He "pleads or appeals" on our behalf, for our good) 24-7, 365 days a year. That means *King Jesus is always in the stands of your life with a foam #1 finger and a handmade sign with your name on it, cheering Himself hoarse!* And on the days you've really mucked it up and don't deserve His support in the stands because you've done something really bad—on the days you've fallen flat on your face—remember He doesn't leave the stadium. He prays and pleads and stands in the gap on your behalf to help you get back up and take the next right step.

So go ahead, tell Him your corniest joke three or four times in a row today or ask Him to swing you around in the front yard like your dad did when you were a kid or be honest with Him about any recent failing, and your heart might just hear either a faint, supernatural chuckle or a tender, "I got you." Because He does. And He always will.

- **WHEN YOU LOOK** back over your life, who has consistently been in your corner? What does it feel like to have an advocate like that?

- **WHEN YOU IMAGINE** Jesus looking at you, do you picture Him smiling, indifferent, or scowling? What is triggered in your mind and heart if you imagine Him cheering over you with an ear-to-ear grin spread across His incarnate face?

Day 16
JESUS AND THE WORD
ARE SUPERNATURALLY SYMBIOTIC

In the beginning was the Word, and the Word was with God,
and the Word was God. JOHN 1:1

MY MIND IS TOO dinky to fully comprehend the supernatural conundrum of how Jesus Christ and the Word are equivalent. It's like theological calculus. But somehow my heart knows it. My heart deeply resonates with the stories on Scripture's paper-thin pages and intuitively knows the Bible isn't something to simply memorize and pull inspirational memes for social media from, nor is it something to weaponize against certain image-bearers I don't agree with. Instead, these enscripturated promises and parameters are divinely enmeshed with the unconditional love of Christ and have the power to pull sinners into a real relationship!

About twenty-five years ago, when I was still a wet-behind-the-ears Bible teacher, I was invited to teach at a women's conference in East Tennessee. Although the event was small, with maybe 150 women in attendance, God used it to change the trajectory of my life and ministry in huge ways. It was an all-day Saturday conference, and as the women were filing into the sanctuary to begin the program, one woman in particular caught my attention. She caught my attention for several reasons: she got there late, she didn't sit down in one of the empty rows at the back of the church and instead remained standing near the door as if she wasn't sure whether she was going to stay or slip out, she reeked of cigarette smoke, and she was wearing a very form-fitting dress with wild "Stevie Nicks-ish" hair instead of the traditional Baptist pouf.

Based on her attire and her reticence to join the rest of the group, I assumed she'd be gone by the afternoon session. But nope, there she was, still in the very back of the church after lunch. I was more than a little surprised when she raised her hand privately when I asked if anyone wanted to put their hope and faith in Jesus. Then I had the pure joy of praying with her when she did. After we prayed, Debbie (not her real name) shyly shared her story.

She explained how she'd grown up with a father who knocked her around and sexually abused her when he got drunk, which was often. By middle school, she'd turned to alcohol and drugs to numb her pain. Tragically, as is often the case with young women whose innocence is stolen by an abusive father or father-figure, she soon fell into the arms of abusive boyfriends because they were familiar and felt like home. And before she'd even graduated from high school, one of them introduced her to prostitution and became her pimp. The next few years were a blur of working as a waitress by day and working in solicitation at night.

A few years later, a young Christian woman who was about her age and pregnant began frequenting the restaurant where Debbie worked as a waitress and made it her mission to get to know her. She always asked to be seated in her section, left generous tips, and then let Debbie hold her baby boy after he was born. Debbie told me softly, "I assumed Miss Carol knew what my night job was because we live in a small town and most people know what I do because I've been busted for solicitation several times. But it didn't seem to bother her because she just kept coming and sitting at my table once or twice a week with her little boy, and within a few years he started drawing me pictures that I put on my refrigerator. I almost convinced myself they were my family because no one had ever been so nice to me."

Debbie's unlikely friendship with Carol is how she ended up at the conference for which I was teaching on that fateful day. Because Carol had invited her and wouldn't take no for an answer! Once Carol paid for her ticket and hand-delivered it, Debbie relented although she felt anxious and uncomfortable because she hadn't been inside a church since she was a child. She confessed that her plan was to make a quick appearance at the beginning of the event and then slip out after saying hi to Carol. But she said after I started talking, she was intrigued because I wasn't the kind of "church lady" she'd envisioned. After I told an embarrassing story on myself and said something about how perfection isn't a prerequisite for a real relationship with God, she decided to stay for a little while because I wasn't too boring. (Some days are better than others!)

She said she was stunned when I started teaching from Hosea and told the story about a woman in the Bible named Gomer who was a *prostitute*. She said, "I'd never heard that story before, Lisa. I had no idea there was somebody like me in the Good Book. And hearing you talk about how God loved her made me think that maybe He could love me too."

I still think about Debbie almost every time I have the undeserved privilege of opening my Bible and talking about Jesus with people at events, conferences, and churches anywhere in the world. Largely because of her, I still believe the "Yes, Jesus loves me" refrain in our hearts and minds will get loud enough to change the world around us when we better understand, appreciate, and trust the "For the Bible tells me so" part!

- **DO YOU READ** God's Word more out of discipline or delight?

- **WHAT PASSAGES OR** stories help you lean more fully into the love of Jesus? Why do you think you resonate with them so much? In what ways do they give you a little bit more courage to explore the less-familiar parts of the Bible?

Day 17

JESUS HOLDS OUT HOPE FOR US

Dear friends, don't overlook this one fact: With the Lord one day is like a thousand years, and a thousand years like one day. The Lord does not delay his promise, as some understand delay, but is patient with you, not wanting any to perish but all to come to repentance. 2 PETER 3:8–9

NOT TOO LONG AGO, I went back to a crack house where I spent a lot of time about ten years ago when I was in the process of adopting the unborn baby of a young woman who lived there. She was a hard-core addict, worked as a prostitute, and was mentally challenged as the result of severe abuse she'd experienced at the hands of her birth parents—who were both heroin addicts—when she was just a baby. Needless to say, I quickly found myself every bit as concerned about this pregnant image-bearer (who was young enough to be my daughter) as I was concerned about the child she was carrying. And while I was completely devastated when the adoption fell through at the eleventh hour (four days before I was supposed to bring the baby home), I often still think about and pray for them both.

I hoped she wouldn't be there when I knocked on that all-too-familiar dilapidated door. I hoped maybe she'd finally agreed to go to rehab. Maybe she'd gotten clean and gotten a job serving fast food instead of serving up her petite, track-marked body to abusive johns. Unfortunately, that's not what happened. After I pounded on the door for several minutes, it cracked open to reveal her scowling new pimp and his growling pit bull. When I calmly assured him that I was an old friend of hers and not an undercover cop, he swung the door all the way open and gestured dismissively toward her with an expletive.

She was sprawled out on the same threadbare couch I remembered and was obviously high because her eyes were unfocused and her head was lolling from side to side. I softly told her who I was, that I still loved her, and asked if she needed any help. She mumbled she didn't remember me and was waiting for a "boyfriend"—which meant her pimp was about to hand her over to some stranger to do whatever he wanted with her in exchange for fifteen or twenty dollars. Then she asked groggily if I could loan her a few bucks because she really needed another hit. My heart broke with fresh sorrow as I walked away from that precious girl in that dreadful shack. When I told my friends and family where I'd been, they asked why in the world I went back to the place that was the genesis of so much pain all those years ago. And I told them I'm holding out hope that one day she won't be there anymore.

I don't think disappointment or even anguish when our journey seems especially long is what distances us from God. I believe hopelessness does. Which is why I love Peter's reminder that apathy is not in our Savior's emotional repertoire. Jesus is not slow in keeping His promises; any perceived delay on our end is rooted in His divine patience. As we see clearly from the passage, Jesus has a reason for why He has waited so long to return to the world and deal with all that has gone wrong in it: He's holding out for those who will eventually come to repentance. He's waiting for the many wayward souls who will finally be restored to His Father at some point between today and that Final Day. He's not slow! He's long-suffering as He holds out hope for the lost—and the found. If this is how He treats those who don't know Him yet, how certain should we be of His patience with those of us who because of His amazing grace already have a relationship with Him?

- **HAVE YOU EVER** been afraid that God was losing patience with you? If so, why?

- **IF THE REASON** He waits to return in His second coming is because He's waiting patiently for more wayward, unbelieving people to be saved and restored to Him, what does that tell you about the way He treats your wayward seasons now that you're already one of His children?

- **IN LOOKING BACK** over your life, do you notice any "delays" that seemed especially difficult at the time but now reflect His compassion? How has this changed your outlook on current delays?

Day 18
JESUS IS WORTH WHATEVER IT COSTS

After Jesus was born in Bethlehem of Judea in the days of King Herod, wise men from the east arrived in Jerusalem, saying, "Where is he who has been born king of the Jews? For we saw his star at its rising and have come to worship him." MATTHEW 2:1–2

WHEN I WAS FIVE years old, my older sister, Theresa, explained to me that Santa was a myth, logically using the fact that our home in Florida didn't have a chimney in which he could descend with the presents as proof that the whole "jolly fellow in a red velvet suit" thing was a farce. I, of course, went to bed that night devastated. But I woke up with a jolt several hours later to the sound of hooves and jingle bells on the roof directly over my head, followed by a very loud, "Ho, Ho, Ho!" I bolted out of bed and raced into the living room where my mom was sitting calmly on the couch, and proclaimed enthusiastically, *"Mama, Santa is ON OUR ROOF!"* She responded, "I know, honey." Then she told me to hurry back to bed before he saw me. And my belief in Santa Claus was restored for another season.

I was ready to receive the truth about Mr. Claus the following year at six. But I didn't find out it was my mom's baby sister, Aunt Darlene, who'd clomped across the roof masquerading as Santa until I was a teenager. And by then the fact that she'd climbed up on our roof despite her extreme fear of heights because she wanted to help restore my shattered childhood hope was even sweeter to me than the fictional account about the fat guy with flying reindeer!

At the risk of messing with your favorite nativity scene that's lovingly displayed each December, we're going to explore some facts about the wise men that will hopefully be sweeter to you than the fictional account about them. Their moniker "wise men" comes from the Greek word, *magoi*, from which we get the English transliteration *magi*. They were from Persia/modern-day Iran, and contrary to tradition and holiday lawn ornaments, there weren't actually *three* of them (notice how our passage today simply says "wise men from the east," with no mention of how many). The number three was adopted in early Christian culture in light of the trio of gifts they brought Jesus, not a number that was historically ascribed to their Middle Eastern men's club! Furthermore, those lovely lyrics bellowed at Christmas Eve candlelight services the world over, "We three kings of Orient are," aren't factual either because there are no records of them being royal. They were wise, but the Bible doesn't say they were kings.

What we do know about these wise guys is that they witnessed an astral phenomenon (some scholars surmise it was a comet) prophesied about in the Old Testament (Num. 24:17). I think it's really interesting that rabbinic legend says that on the night Abraham (who we know as the father of Judaism, Christianity, and Islam) was born in Mesopotamia, there was also an unusually radiant astral projection seen by wise men known as Nimrod's astrologers.[13] If that's true, then that would mean a bright star wouldn't be seen as some new thing; rather, something that had a storied past and deep meaning in ancient history—which would make a lot of sense of why these magi dropped everything to follow it.

Since the journey from their homeland in Persia to Israel is more than one thousand miles (which would've taken them a long time to walk/ride camels), they don't belong in nativity scenes alongside the shepherds. They couldn't possibly have made it to Jerusalem for Jesus's birth in time. But when they finally—after slogging through seemingly endless sandy miles and then being detained by a paranoid nutjob named King Herod—found themselves in front of the Christ child, they fell on their knees in worship and were both overwhelmed and overjoyed!

Then, when they recovered enough to remember their manners, they gave Jesus three very costly gifts: gold, frankincense, and myrrh, each of which has symbolic significance.

- *Gold* was (and still is) very expensive and was used extensively in the making of temple religious objects and furniture to represent royalty.

- *Frankincense* is an incense or perfumed oil that's harvested by slicing a rare tree from the genus *Boswellia* (these trees are still found in Southern Arabia and Somalia) and then collecting the milky white resin, which is where the name comes from because the Semitic root word of frankincense means "white" or "pure."

- *Myrrh* comes from the bark of a small, especially odiferous tree and it was mingled with wine to be used as an anesthetic and was also used in preparing a body for burial.

In short, gold symbolized the kingliness of Jesus because of its value. Frankincense symbolized that He wasn't just a random king, but God, to whom worship is due because it was the purest incense burned in the temple. And myrrh symbolized Jesus's humanity because it could be used to make His pain on the cross less dreadful and His burial less repulsive. *King. God. Human. All wrapped into one.* A person like that is worth any and every gift we could bestow!

I don't have a set of wise men in the nativity scene I carefully arrange on a side table in our living room every year on Thanksgiving afternoon. Instead, I have a custom-made, cast-iron set of magi that I keep on display 365 days a year to help me remember that they left their homes and their jobs and their families to seek the Savior for a very, very long time. (Based on Matthew 2:16, which states that after Herod realized he'd been tricked by the magi he became enraged and decreed that all Jewish males from the age of two and under were to be killed, their journey may have taken *two years*.) In addition, I keep a tiny vial of frankincense oil right next to them as a tangible reminder that nothing I have is too costly a gift for the King who willingly laid down His royal scepter and chose to be born in a barn so that we could be redeemed.

- **HOW LONG WAS** your journey to find Jesus? What and/or whom did you have to leave in order to seek Him?

- **HOW COSTLY HAVE** the gifts been that you've figuratively laid at Jesus's feet? Each of the wise men's gifts conveyed something about Him. What have your gifts, past or present, conveyed about Him?

Day 19

JESUS GIVES EXTRA REST
TO THE MOST EXHAUSTED

"Come to me, all of you who are weary and burdened, and I will give you rest. Take up my yoke and learn from me, because I am lowly and humble in heart, and you will find rest for your souls. For my yoke is easy and my burden is light." MATTHEW 11:28–30

FOR LOTS OF PERSONAL reasons, a large part of this past year was very difficult and draining. In fact, there were multiple times when I felt like I was trudging through wet cement and could barely make any forward progress. Thankfully, I rarely found myself doubting God's mercy. That's the wonderful thing about having history with our Redeemer, because based on over five decades of walking/skipping/limping with Jesus, I've found Him to be especially present during painful seasons. However, I did question the strength and resilience of my own threadbare heart.

But God.

He lifted my head and set my feet on higher ground—literally and figuratively—while Missy and I were at a four-day retreat at the C Lazy U Ranch at the western edge of Rocky Mountain National Park in Colorado. Mind you, my "miracle" didn't happen right away. First of all, we had to deal with a two-hour flight delay out of Nashville. Then our baggage was delayed in Denver, just long enough to cause our rental car reservation to get canceled. After waiting in a snail-paced line and conversing with a frazzled agent (I'd rather dig ditches than be a car rental agent), we finally left the airport in a very squeaky and leaky SUV with high miles four hours *after* we were supposed to be en route to the ranch. By the time we made the two-and-a-half-hour trek up a narrow alpine highway with more curves than a plus-sized model, both John Michael (my nephew) and Missy had altitude sickness. Which was exacerbated by the fact that we didn't drink enough water on the tiresome journey because there were so few places to stop and tinkle! Anyway, by the time we rolled into the ranch we were emotionally dehydrated too.

Of course, the reception desk was closed, so we had to schlep our luggage down a dark, rock-strewn trail to our bunkroom. And the moment we opened the door, I sensed what little cheer was left in my wee family evaporate because it was a petite space, crammed with two towering bunk beds, a tiny bathroom, no place for luggage, and plenty of spiders. Since I was the only parent and aunt present, I quickly felt compelled to say something positive like: "This is going to be such a fun adventure, y'all—I haven't slept on a bunk bed since I was in college!" But when I looked up from what I was doing to smile at Missy and John Michael, I whacked my head *hard* on the top bunk rail, resulting in a sizable goose egg. At which point, my inner Pollyanna bolted for greener pastures, and I mumbled something whiny along the lines of: "Why me, God?" You know that old adage: *Sometimes you have to hit rock bottom before you can look up and see God?* Well, I've resembled that remark a time or two!

My much-needed breakthrough happened on our last day at the ranch when Missy and I got to experience what they call the "jingle," which is when their two hundred and some horses are let loose (no saddles or bridles or riders) to run free on thousands of wide-open acres at sunset each evening. One of the wranglers had encouraged us to hike to the other side of the river and tuck ourselves behind a big wagon where we could watch them race by mere feet away, so we literally felt the ground shake as they thundered past!

In those glorious, dust-filled moments, as I was holding my wide-eyed, horse-obsessed daughter close to me for safety, I sensed our Creator-Redeemer pulling me into His embrace in much the same way. Then, I could almost hear the affectionate chuckle rumbling in His chest when a pair of diminutive donkeys came trotting out well behind the magnificent herd. Which is when our kind King effectively winked at me, pointed at those wee beasts in last place, and said, "Honey, I've always had a soft spot for the scratch-and-dent bin."

For those of you precious saints who feel like you're at the end of the pro-verbial rope, may I encourage you with the reminder that the "knot" of Christ's compassionate faithfulness is sufficient? Based on a half century with Jesus that has been littered with low moments, I can tell you that He's never let my weary head slip below the surface of the waters I thought might drown me. He can easily tote the weight of our heaviest burdens and His are the safest arms in which to collapse. . . . I promise.

- **WHEN'S THE LAST** time you exhaled emotionally and put all your weight on Jesus?

- **WHAT'S STOPPING YOU** from doing that right now?

Day 20

JESUS GIVES SIGHT TO
ALL KINDS OF BLINDNESS

*They brought the man who used to be blind to the Pharisees. The day
that Jesus made the mud and opened his eyes was a Sabbath. Then
the Pharisees asked him again how he received his sight.*

"He put mud on my eyes," he told them. "I washed and I can see."

*Some of the Pharisees said, "This man is not from God, because he
doesn't keep the Sabbath." But others were saying, "How can a sinful man
perform such signs?" And there was a division among them.*

Again they asked the blind man, "What do you say about him, since he opened your eyes?"

"He's a prophet," he said.

*The Jews did not believe this about him—that he was blind and received sight—
until they summoned the parents of the one who had received his sight.*

They asked them, "Is this your son, the one you say was born blind? How then does he now see?"

*"We know this is our son and that he was born blind," his parents answered. "But we don't
know how he now sees, and we don't know who opened his eyes. Ask him; he's of age. He
will speak for himself." His parents said these things because they were afraid of the Jews,
since the Jews had already agreed that if anyone confessed him as the Messiah, he would
be banned from the synagogue. This is why his parents said, "He's of age; ask him."*

*So a second time they summoned the man who had been blind and told
him, "Give glory to God. We know that this man is a sinner."*

*He answered, "Whether or not he's a sinner, I don't know. <u>One thing I do
know: I was blind, and now I can see!</u>"* JOHN 9:13–25, EMPHASIS MINE

THE LAST FEW MONTHS have been emotionally blurry as I've linked arms
with my family and limped through the unexpected death of a first cousin, as
well as the sobering, stage 4 cancer diagnosis of an uncle. Yet because of the
responsibilities of everyday life—deadlines and dinner preparation and doctor
visits (because I got COVID for the second time, although thankfully it wasn't
nearly as serious as my first go-round)—I found myself putting my head down
and just plowing through. You know those seasons you find yourself *enduring*
much more so than *enjoying*?

But then I came face-to-face with pure grace recently when I got to reconnect with a beautiful image-bearer named Lindsey, whom I first met when she was in her early twenties and just starting her addiction recovery journey while facing a possible ten-year prison sentence. God knit us quickly and deeply during a six-month Bible study/hot-mess club I had the undeserved privilege of leading at the faith-based, residential program she was remanded to while awaiting sentencing. Lindsey was, for all intents and purposes, the first young woman I mothered.

However, because of circumstances beyond our control, we lost touch after she graduated from the program and was incarcerated. And yet here she was again, twelve years later, striding toward me at the altar of a church where I was standing after speaking at a women's worship night. She looked almost exactly the same as she did the last time I'd seen her all those years ago—albeit with a more radiant countenance—and was trailed by a lovely gaggle of women whom I soon found out are all residents in the *faith-based addiction recovery program* she and her husband founded after they got out of prison! During our long, tearful, first-of-many embraces, Lindsey whispered, "Everything you prayed over me twelve years ago has come true." There was a time she struggled to see out of the trench she was stuck in—and we've all been there. But now, here she was, eyes wide open and brimming with hope and faith in Jesus. Eyes looking *outward* to others to give them hope, to help them look toward Jesus so they can see out of their trenches too! It took all the restraint I could muster not to collapse into a heaving pile of praise and thanksgiving a few minutes later while watching her and Missy meet for the first time and then hug like long-lost sisters.

Life is sometimes hard and heartbreaking because we live in a broken world marred by sin, but my goodness, there are *So. Many. More. Miracles* yet to be rejoiced over, y'all! So many more treasures of divine grace yet to be dug from the hard clay of our lives. So many more seasons we'll see the glory and redemption of our great God when we were blind to it just one short season ago. Don't you just love being newly slayed by the redemptive kindness of King Jesus? Color me wildly grateful, freshly hopeful, deeply content, and just a teensy bit worn out from our recent revival.

- **WHAT RECENT HARDSHIPS** have dulled or sullied your perspective of Jesus?

- **READ ISAIAH 40:11** (preferably in the New Living Translation or The Message paraphrase). How does your perspective change when you ponder the promise of God holding us close to His heart?

Day 21

JESUS USES RELATIONSHIPS FOR REDEMPTIVE PURPOSES

But the word of the Lord came to me: "You have shed much blood and waged great wars. You are not to build a house for my name because you have shed so much blood on the ground before me. But a son will be born to you; he will be a man of rest. I will give him rest from all his surrounding enemies, for his name will be Solomon, and I will give peace and quiet to Israel during his reign. He is the one who will build a house for my name. He will be my son, and I will be his father. I will establish the throne of his kingdom over Israel forever." 1 CHRONICLES 22:8–10

ALTHOUGH I'VE NEVER WORKED as a shepherd or felled an evil giant with a slingshot, much less served as God's chosen royal sovereign over a nation, I can identify with King David. Like him, I fell in love with God when I was little. And like him, I also betrayed my first love and chose my wants over His will. And while I've never had literal blood on my hands, I know all too well what it feels like to carry such heavy shame that I couldn't get past the blueprint stage of dreams I desperately hoped to build.

Today's passage (don't worry, we'll still get to a promissory passage about Jesus even though it wasn't at the top like normal!) reveals that King David was not allowed to build the temple even though he was a man after God's own heart (1 Sam. 13:14) because there'd been too much blood on his hands as a military leader. God had chosen someone else to build His house: David's son, Solomon. These words from God came across as sad and even a bit punitive to me for years. But when I became a mom, I began to read them from a different perspective, ultimately with deep, resonating gratitude.

I explained this story to Missy recently and told her that if Jesus tarries, much like Solomon, she'll build more incredible things for God than I ever could because she won't carry the debilitating weight of things she wasn't built for. Said another way, as one generation turns to the next, she'll be able to take up the mantle of God's call without all the baggage I would have brought to the table should I have been the one to answer the call God has on *her* life. And I'm increasingly confident about my daughter having a bondage-free future because of the saints God has graciously woven into our tiny family's story to serve as her spiritual aunts and uncles. Dear friends who are willing to dislocate their proverbial shoulders in order to make supernatural doorways wider for Missy to walk through.

We weren't made to walk alone, y'all. God made us in His trinitarian, communal image (Gen. 1:26–27), which means *we're divinely wired for relationship*! We're called to cultivate friends who are safe and mature enough to know about the "blood" that's been on our hands in the past, yet who still passionately believe and pray for redemptive miracles in our future. Who could even take up the mantle in the very place we need to lay it down. Who help pull off God's vast purposes in this world as a team, *together*, one generation after the next. Do whatever it takes to surround yourself with a community of honest believers who are preoccupied with loving God and other image-bearers. Listen for times when the Lord might be calling them to enter in and take up the torch in the places you need time to recover, rest, or repent from past blood on your hands. Choose to remember that it takes *all* of us to build everything that God wants to build in this world. Press into people who are planted firmly in Jesus— especially the ones who come right before you and right after you (for this is how God's work is carried forward!)—and He promises to be right there in the middle of your motley crew.

> "Again, truly I tell you, if two of you on earth agree about any matter that you pray for, it will be done for you by my Father in heaven. For where two or three are gathered together in my name, I am there among them." (Matt. 18:19–20)

- **READ ECCLESIASTES 3:1–8** and also 4:9–12. How would you synopsize each of these passages in your own words?

- **PROVERBS 27:17 (NLT)** proclaims: "As iron sharpens iron, so a friend sharpens a friend." What faithful friend(s) can you trust to consistently point you toward Jesus?

Day 22
JESUS ADVOCATES UNITY, NOT UNIFORMITY

For just as the body is one and has many parts, and all the parts of that body, though many, are one body—so also is Christ. For we were all baptized by one Spirit into one body—whether Jews or Greeks, whether slaves or free—and we were all given one Spirit to drink. Indeed, the body is not one part but many. If the foot should say, "Because I'm not a hand, I don't belong to the body," it is not for that reason any less a part of the body. And if the ear should say, "Because I'm not an eye, I don't belong to the body," it is not for that reason any less a part of the body. If the whole body were an eye, where would the hearing be? If the whole body were an ear, where would the sense of smell be? But as it is, God has arranged each one of the parts in the body just as he wanted. And if they were all the same part, where would the body be? As it is, there are many parts, but one body. The eye cannot say to the hand, "I don't need you!" Or again, the head can't say to the feet, "I don't need you!" On the contrary, those parts of the body that are weaker are indispensable. And those parts of the body that we consider less honorable, we clothe these with greater honor, and our unrespectable parts are treated with greater respect, which our respectable parts do not need. 1 CORINTHIANS 12:12–24A, EMPHASIS MINE

I'M A MIDDLE-AGED, THEOLOGICALLY conservative Bible teacher, who rides a motorcycle in black leather pants. I'm also a single, Caucasian woman with chemically dependent hair whom God graciously chose to become the undeserved, adoptive mom to an extraordinary toddler from Haiti named Missy, who's now matured into a middle-schooler with gorgeous curly hair. I'm not tied to one particular denominational stream of the Christian faith—as long as we can agree on the reality of the Trinity; the authority of Scripture; and the sole, atoning sufficiency of Jesus Christ's sacrifice for our salvation and reconciliation with God, I'm happy as a clam. Which means, I don't fit most Bible teacher stereotypes and am sometimes viewed as a square peg in some of the rounder Christian circles. That used to trouble me in my people-pleasing past, but not so much anymore. It's taken a long time, but I finally trust that most of my uniqueness was divinely designed.

I believe our triune God wired me to love Jesus with all my heart and to love my daughter, Missy, above everyone on this planet apart from Him. He also fashioned me a chatty extrovert who thoroughly enjoys being part of authentic, perfectly imperfect communities—that is, places and spaces filled with people who really matter to each other even when they get on each other's last nerve!

I think He knit my tongue and mind together in such a symbiotic way that I love telling stories, especially stories that come from the Bible's metanarrative of grace and highlight His compassion. He filled me with ingredients that, when shaken and stirred, cause me to love laughing and teasing with friends and family. And He gave me a double portion of fondness for nature, adventure, and literature because I love being outside in His stunningly beautiful Creation. I prefer crickets to car horns, flip-flops to high heels and a ball cap on a ski boat to a ball gown on a yacht. I'm also an enthusiastic participant of all things gardening, biking, hiking, swimming, skiing, and reading. I really, really like to read!

While I often talk more than I listen, He also put that still, small voice called Holy Spirit in my head who constantly reminds me of how our heavenly Father gave me two ears and one mouth for a reason! I know my Redeemer understands my fear of snakes—even the "harmless" ones—in light of all the sinful brouhaha that went down in Eden because of a slithery, lying, rotten fruit salesmen kind of serpent. And I think He also understands why I stopped listening to telemarketers' pitches (who sometimes, in some small way, remind me of the creepy crawler in that first garden) because He knows that deep down I want to be more healthy and less motivated by guilt (yet I still feel a little guilty about hanging up on them).

I can sense Him tagging along on long, meandering rides or hikes with Missy. And I can sense His sorrow over how hard it is for me to trust someone with my whole heart because of past wounds. I feel His pleasure while wiggling during musical worship. (Which has made for an awkward moment or two during visits to less-expressive churches, but when we're singing about Jesus, I feel like I have helium balloons tied to my hands—they just have to go up!)

It's probably not completely righteous like the anger He displayed when He flipped those trashy, mercenary, money changers' tables outside the temple, but I can feel Jesus regulating the indignation that rises up in me when someone is unkind to my daughter or any other child, for that matter. It is a microscopic measure of His wisdom that fuels my passion for the theological principle of *imago Dei,* which means that every single person regardless of gender, ethnicity, culture, socioeconomic status, mental capacity, or physical ability was made in God's image—whether they acknowledge Jesus as their Savior or not—and is, therefore, inherently worthy of dignity and respect. I can barely stomach people who are cruel or condescending to others for *any* reason.

I hear His gentle rebuke in my heart when I accidentally say words that aren't in the Bible when I think I'm about to run into another car or they're about to ram into me. And I notice His gentle "thumbs-up" when I'm being honest about my many frailties and insecurities. More than that, I sense His super strong "thumbs-up"—or perhaps I should call it outright delight!—when I surrender those insecurities and choose to use both *all* my wiring and *all* the gifts He's given me for the edification of His church.

Why do I share all of this? To offer a monologue on all the things you could have gone without knowing about me? To shout to the world that clearly my role in the body of Christ is to be the belly? Or maybe the mouth? No sirree! While I very well might be the belly or the mouth (and I'm down with both!), I shared all this to model what it looks like to know who *exactly* you are and how God made you, not just in this great big world, but in the body of Christ! And moreover, to stop apologizing for it and to start *using* it for His glory!

Jesus didn't just save me. He also equipped me to be part of a whole so that others might lean more fully into Him or even launch themselves into His unconditionally loving embrace for the first time. And the same goes for you. So what part of the body are *you*? How are *you* made? What parts of yourself have you been hiding from or apologizing for, when you could use them instead for the good of your neighbors and your fellow Christians? Don't rob others of the gifts Jesus has given you—He made you a certain way for a reason! (And if you've never tried, follow today's devotional as a guide. Try writing five or six paragraphs about who you really are and when you most feel God's pleasure, conviction, or power.)

- **WHAT PART OF** the symbolic body of faith Paul describes in 1 Corinthians 12 do you most identify with and why?

- **WHAT RELATIVELY UNIQUE** and—best you can tell—God-given characteristics do you have that tend to increase the compassion and efficacy in a community of Christ-followers? Explain what and how.

- **ARE THERE ANY** specific gifts Jesus has given you that you aren't currently using? Why? How might you take a step toward sharing your gifts this week?

Day 23
JESUS IS MAKING ALL THINGS NEW

Then the one seated on the throne said, "Look, I am making everything new." He also said, "Write, because these words are faithful and true." Then he said to me, "It is done! I am the Alpha and the Omega, the beginning and the end. I will freely give to the thirsty from the spring of the water of life." REVELATION 21:5–6

ONE NIGHT, WHEN MISSY was eight years old, she pulled up a stool next to me at the kitchen island where I was working on my laptop and said with precious resolution, "Mama, I'm ready to give my heart to Jesus now, so will you help me?" Of course, I wanted to jump for joy and run laps around the yard while bellowing, "My baby girl is launching herself into the arms of Jesus RIGHT. NOW. y'all!" Thankfully, the Holy Spirit nudged me to dial back the zeal a smidge, so I didn't sully her precious sincerity! We talked for a while before I had the incomparable privilege of praying with my daughter, whom I don't remotely deserve, to give her heart to Jesus. And I would probably *still* be in the honeymoon stage of that moment had it not been for what she declared immediately after she said amen, which was: "Mama, I'm so happy I gave my heart to Jesus, but I don't want to get baptized yet because I don't really understand it."

I was a tad flustered by her admission, but after I mulled over it for a minute, I realized how wise Missy's hesitancy was and I assured her the Holy Spirit would let her know when the time was right. A few months passed before she declared herself ready to be baptized, which she then qualified with the enthusiastic proclamation: "And Momma, I want to be baptized *IN THE JORDAN RIVER!*"

I was so tickled by her animated innocence—and the fact that the significance of the Jordan River mattered to her—but I thought: *Yikes, a trip overseas to Israel for her baptism is a lot more complicated than scheduling it with our pastoral care team at church!* Of course, I didn't share that with Missy because I didn't want to pour cold water (no pun intended) on her newly awakened spiritual passion, but I secretly wondered how in the world I could make a dunk in our local baptistry as meaningful to her as a trip to Jesus's baptismal site.

But wouldn't you know it, a few days later I got an invitation to help lead a tour of Israel with Lifeway because more people than they expected had registered for the trip, so they needed a second Bible teacher! Truly, only God. And it just kept getting better! Because we already had another international trip preceding the Israel tour, Missy and I ended up arriving in Jerusalem a day and a half behind everybody else, and the very first holy site we were able to join the group at was the Jordan River! Plus, we didn't intercept them at the lovely, touristy setting on the northern shore of the Sea of Galilee part of the river either; instead, the timing and itinerary worked out for us to rendezvous with the tour at the spot below the southern shore where the Jordan basically bottlenecks before it flows into the Dead Sea. For context, this is the spot where that stream—arguably the most symbolically significant water in the entire Bible—is muddy due to agricultural runoff and perhaps just a teensy bit of sewage, according to recent reports by advocates for clean water!

Partly because she was exhausted from the twenty-three hours of travel it took for us to get there, and partly because it was cold and rainy, but mostly because that brown water looked so nasty and uninviting, Missy began to backpedal regarding the enthusiastic proclamation she'd made months before about wanting to be baptized in the Jordan River.

But after I explained that even though it wasn't the picturesque site most tourists get baptized in when they visit Israel, *it was the very place* that the Israelites crossed over the Jordan into the Promised Land after forty years of wandering around in the wilderness; and *it was the very place* where God sent a supernatural Uber chariot to whisk Elijah into heaven; and *it was the very place Johnny B baptized Jesus* and God's Spirit descended like a dove fluttering down to seal the deal while the Father bellowed, "You are my beloved Son; with you I am well-pleased" (Mark 1:11), she ultimately relented and let me dunk her all the way under while an enthusiastic crowd of onlookers from all over the world celebrated with us! Watching her come up out of that holy water, shaking droplets from her beautiful curls, made every dark night and dry season of waiting for a miracle absolutely worth it.

During this middle season, between the "already" of Jesus's first coming and the "not yet" of His second, we must not forget the fact that Jesus is still actively involved in the process of redemption . . . of making all things new.

- **WHAT UNFULFILLED HOPES** and dreams are you still waiting on for God to "complete"?

- **READ PHILIPPIANS 1:6,** James 5:7–8, and Revelation 21:1–4. How can these Scriptures help you hang onto Jesus's promise about making all things new?

Day 24

JESUS IS A RESTORER OF ALL THAT
SEEMS IRREPARABLY BROKEN

*So the crowd was amazed when they saw those unable to speak talking,
the crippled <u>restored</u>, the lame walking, and the blind seeing, and they
gave glory to the God of Israel.* MATTHEW 15:31, EMPHASIS MINE

THE DAY AFTER MISSY'S baptism, I experienced another better-than-I-could've-dreamt moment when Missy and I approached the Western Wall and placed a slip of paper on which I'd written a prayer into a crack. You probably know the magnitude of the Western Wall (often called the "Wailing Wall"); it is located in the Old City of Jerusalem and was originally part of the temple structure erected by Herod the Great, and since the destruction of the temple in AD 70, it's the only segment of that sacred structure left where Jews can gather to pray. Therefore, it's customary for them to come to the wall to grieve the downfall of the temple and the Holy City and to pray for their restoration. The tearful laments of devotees are usually uttered with their foreheads pressed against those giant, Herodian stones and often accompanied by the act of placing small prayer scrolls in the cracks and crevices of the wall to commemorate their petitions.[14]

The first time I had the sober privilege of placing a small slip of paper inscribed with a prayer into the Western Wall was in 1998 on a trip with Kay Arthur, but I can't remember my request. The second time I gently poked a plea in between those ancient stones was in late September of 2000 on the day before Yom Kippur—the highest holy day in the Jewish calendar—and I vividly remember that request. I was approaching forty and still single, but I felt like God had healed much of the shame and relational toxicity that had reigned in my heart since childhood. So I decided to be as brave and vulnerable as I could, and I wrote a prayer thanking God for my healing and asking that, if it wasn't too late, I would love for Him to please give me a family of my own.

There were a thousand praises dancing in my heart in light of His extravagant grace as I approached the Western Wall for a third time on April 1, 2019, while holding my daughter's hand, nineteen years after asking Him for a family of my own. But there were only two words written on the prayer I let Missy nudge into a tiny fissure: *Thank You.* Somehow that short phrase said it all.

The older I get—and sixty is right around the corner, y'all!—the more often I find myself pondering how patient our God is when it comes to restoring what's broken in our world and in our lives. He consistently weaves divine grace into the messy milieu of humanity even though we're prone to wander and rebuff His reno plans time after time. I had the joy of hanging out with a few women who are residents of a faith-based recovery center recently, and all of them confessed that it wasn't their first attempt at getting clean. One precious, raspy-voiced, stumbling saint told me it was her sixth time in rehab because she's found it excruciatingly difficult to break her addiction to meth. She said, "Miss Lisa, I hurt every single person who ever loved me so much, they all ended up walking away. Except Jesus. He's the only one I haven't run out of second chances with."

Long after we'd hugged and said goodbye, I kept thinking about what she said: *Jesus is the only one I haven't run out of second chances with.* My bad choices had different consequences; I didn't lose my teeth to meth or my job to alcohol. I've never been incarcerated. But I know what it feels like to be trapped by repetitive rebellion, to sabotage my own healing and wonder if I'll get another chance because I've blown so many. And I found myself crying with fresh gratitude over the fact that our Savior's restorative compassion isn't reserved for jars of clay with clean fractures that are easily repaired with a squirt or two of super-glue. Instead, He lovingly leans down and picks up every single shard of what appears to be irreparably shattered. Then He tenderly puts us back together, piece by piece. Unlike insurance carriers, Jesus doesn't do total write-offs.

- **WHAT BROKEN SITUATIONS,** dreams, or relationships has Jesus already restored in your life story?

- **HOW COULD GRATITUDE—THANKING** Jesus for what He's already fixed—keep us from losing our faith over the situations, dreams, and relationships He has yet to restore? What are some specific things Jesus has fixed in your life over the years?

Day 25

JESUS WILL NEVER LET GO OF US

"My sheep hear my voice, I know them, and they follow me. I give them eternal life, and they will never perish. <u>No one will snatch them out of my hand</u>. My Father, who has given them to me, is greater than all. No one is able to snatch them out of the Father's hand. I and the Father are one." JOHN 10:27–30, EMPHASIS MINE

ONE OF THE FIRST rules I established when Missy's adoption was finalized, and I finally got to bring her home was that she had to hold my hand when we were walking anywhere cars were present. This rule applied to parking lots, city sidewalks, or even along some peaceful path in a suburban neighborhood. I was a stickler about enforcing the policy too. Missy grew up in a very rural Haitian village, so she had limited experience with traffic or the fatal damage automobiles can do when they come into contact with flesh and bone. But since my child is a wonderfully feisty and independent leader, she sometimes balked at the holding-mom's-hand guideline, wanting instead to run ahead of me. So, I called a family meeting between the two of us and employed the use of the word *pancake*. It's one of the few English words Missy understood at the time and a term that had quickly become dear to her because, much like her adoptive mama, my kid's a big fan of carbs!

Once I had her complete attention by getting the pancake mix out of the pantry, stirring the necessary ingredients together, and pouring the first soon-to-be-edible circle on a hot griddle, I said, "Missy, do you want a pancake?" Of course, she nodded enthusiastically and exclaimed, *"Oui, manman blan!"* (*"Yes, white mama"* in Creole.)

While she was happily munching her second-favorite breakfast food (sausage biscuits are the love of her life and remain firmly in the coveted number-one position), I explained that the reason I make her hold my hand in the parking lot at Target, on the way to school, and when we're walking around downtown is because she's little, so drivers have a harder time seeing her than they do a bigger, taller person like me. Then, much to her surprise, I took another pancake off the griddle and plopped it directly on the table in front of her plate. Then I soberly said, "Honey, if a driver doesn't see you and runs over you with their car or truck, you'll be *squashed flat* just like this pancake." My sweet baby girl looked stunned for a moment, then sadly mumbled through a mouthful of food, "I don't wanna be a pancake, Mama."

I didn't make up some dogma about hand-holding around cars in an attempt to squeeze all the gleeful-running-ahead-of-mama fun out of my daughter's day. I did so because I love her more than I knew I had the capacity to love, and I'll do *everything* in my power to protect her. Oh how much more Jesus loves us and is concerned about our welfare! Just marinate for a few minutes in our Creator-Redeemer's protective proclamations, only this time in the easy-to-understand vernacular of The Message paraphrase:

> My sheep recognize my voice. I know them, and they follow me. I give them real and eternal life. *They are protected from the Destroyer for good. No one can steal them from out of my hand. The Father who put them under my care is so much greater than the Destroyer and Thief.* No one could ever get them away from him. (John 10:27–30a, emphasis mine)

> "If anyone attacks you,
>   don't for a moment suppose that I sent them,
> And if any should attack, nothing will come of it.
> I create the blacksmith
>   who fires up his forge
>   and makes a weapon designed to kill.
> I also create the destroyer—
>   but no weapon that can hurt you has ever been forged.
> Any accuser who takes you to court
>   will be dismissed as a liar.
> This is what GOD's servants can expect.
>   I'll see to it that everything works out for the best."
> (Isa. 54:15–17 MSG)

No matter where you go, He's got you. Nothing or no one can snatch you out of His hand. No weapon formed against you will prosper. His commands are always for your good, to protect you, and His guiding hand over your life ensures that you will never, ever end up like a pancake!

- **WHAT IS POTENTIALLY** the most dangerous or scary situation in your life right now?

- **BESIDES PRAYER, WHAT** are some practical ways you can proverbially hold God's hand in the midst of it?

- **WHAT INSTRUCTIONS OF** God seem hard for you to obey right now, but if you really thought about it, could actually be ways He is protecting you from harm?

JESUS'S STORIES HIGHLIGHTED
THE HEART OF THE FATHER

He also said to them, "Suppose one of you has a friend and goes to him at midnight and says to him, 'Friend, lend me three loaves of bread, because a friend of mine on a journey has come to me, and I don't have anything to offer him.' Then he will answer from inside and say, 'Don't bother me! The door is already locked, and my children and I have gone to bed. I can't get up to give you anything.' I tell you, even though he won't get up and give him anything because he is his friend, yet because of his friend's shameless boldness, he will get up and give him as much as he needs.

"So I say to you, ask, and it will be given to you. Seek, and you will find. Knock, and the door will be opened to you. For everyone who asks receives, and the one who seeks finds, and to the one who knocks, the door will be opened. What father among you, if his son asks for a fish, will give him a snake instead of a fish? Or if he asks for an egg, will give him a scorpion? If you then, who are evil, know how to give good gifts to your children, how much more will the heavenly Father give the Holy Spirit to those who ask him?" LUKE 11:5–13

OVER TWO THOUSAND RABBINIC parables exist,[15] and they're scattered throughout a wide variety of both ancient and modern writings. During His earthly ministry, Jesus taught around forty (there's some theological dispute about whether the form of a few of His stories can be formally classified as a parable, but the consensus is that He taught somewhere between thirty-six and forty-two of them in Matthew, Mark, and Luke; note that the Gospel of John doesn't contain any parabolic material).[16] In fact, if you were to go through the Gospels and count all the red-letter words, you'll find that parables make up the bulk of Jesus's preaching material! This drowsy-daddy/rude-neighbor story in Luke 11 has long been one of my favorites, but it became even more so after an experience Missy and I had in Montana a few years ago.

We got to visit Montana in the summer of 2020 because I had the undeserved privilege of speaking at a church in the city of Kalispell. It was the first time Missy and I had flown since the COVID quarantines began in March of 2020, and in light of our super-early departure out of Nashville and a flight delay in Chicago, we were both dragging a bit by the time we got to Big Sky Country. Since my work itinerary didn't start until the next morning, I suggested we go for a short hike to get some fresh air and stretch our legs, which Missy wasn't excited about. She also pooh-poohed my suggestions about walking down to the lake, exploring the quaint downtown area, or even going for a swim in the hotel's heated indoor pool. After a few minutes of silence, I asked, "Honey, am I getting on your nerves?" To which Missy replied *yes* and then added, "Does that hurt your feelings, Mom?"

I assured her that my feelings weren't hurt and that it was *totally normal* to be bugged by your mama, especially when you're tired, jet-lagged, and let's not forget trying to navigate the turbulent waters of puberty. Then I said, "How about we make an imaginary line down the middle of the room—that can be your side, and this will be my side—and I'll just stay on my side and study for the next few hours and you can stay on that side and read or do homework on your iPad and we don't have to talk unless you want to?" She agreed and we stayed in that pleasant-but-separate arrangement until both of us got ready for bed and turned out the light. But after a few minutes of silence in that dark hotel room, Missy whispered, "Mama, will you please cross the line and cuddle me, because I don't think I can fall asleep if you don't rub my back first." She didn't have to bang on the door to get my attention . . . all my precious daughter had to do was whisper!

The two main characters in this story Jesus tells are the sleeping father and the impudent friend trying to rouse him for a midnight snack. The father, of course, symbolizes God the Father—which is almost always the case when Jesus includes a father figure in a parable—and while there's no theological consensus regarding who the persistent neighbor represents, one of my professors at Denver Seminary, Dr. Craig Blomberg (who's considered to be one of the world's foremost authorities on the parables!), teaches that he symbolizes unbelievers. Those who live outside of the household of God.

But then there's an oft-overlooked tertiary character: the children. And because this parable takes place in the context of first-century Semitic culture, it's safe to assume they would've been snuggled up in bed right next to their dad because most homes in that era only had one room for sleeping, and children typically slept with their parents. With that in mind, let's take another look at the tail end of this tale:

> "Which of you fathers, if your son asks for a fish, will give him a snake instead? Or if he asks for an egg, will give him a scorpion? If

you then, though you are evil, know how to give good gifts to your children, how much more will your Father in heaven give the Holy Spirit to those who ask him!" (Luke 11:11–13 NIV)

Our omniscient Messiah brilliantly uses *a fortiori* logic—a fancy Latin phrase that means "from the lesser to the greater"—to reveal *how much more* our loving heavenly Father generously gives to His children than a daddy with skin on. If the people *outside* of God's household could bank on His generosity when they were persistent to communicate their needs, those precious peanuts *inside* the household didn't have to bang on the door and twist their Father's arm when they needed another bedtime story, or a glass of water, or a back rub to break the ice; all they had to do was whisper because He was right there next to them the whole time, smiling with twinkly-eyed affection. This parable is most often used to underscore the importance of persistent prayer, but my favorite takeaway is the how-close-our-God-is-to-us part!

- **READ MARK 4:11–12.** Why do you think Jesus used parables to both *conceal* and *reveal*?

- **WHAT IS YOUR** favorite parable and why?

- **IS THERE ANYTHING** you need to ask God for in this season of life? Take some time to do it right now!

Day 27

JESUS IS AN ADVOCATE FOR WOMEN

Afterward he was traveling from one town and village to another, preaching and telling the good news of the kingdom of God. The Twelve were with him, and also some women who had been healed of evil spirits and sicknesses: Mary, called Magdalene (seven demons had come out of her); Joanna the wife of Chuza, Herod's steward; Susanna; and many others who were supporting them from their possessions. LUKE 8:1–3

WHEN JESUS ADDED WOMEN to His entourage, He may as well have poked a hornet's nest with a short stick because, by doing so, He effectively thumbed His divine nose at pervasive misogynistic standards that had been in place for more than a millennia in the ancient Near East. Women being included as disciples in a rabbi's band of pupils wasn't simply a novel concept in this patriarchal period where women were typically disregarded as chattel—as something a man could *own*—it was outrageous.

Furthermore, religious leaders during the earthly ministry of Jesus Christ were beyond complicit when it came to gender discrimination. A familiar rabbinic proverb declared: "It's better that the Torah be burned than it should be taught to a woman."[17] Even more disheartening, the last line of a common prayer that was expected to be recited three times a day by rabbis during the era of Christ is: *"Praised be Thou, O Lord, who did not make me a woman."*[18] Josephus, a famous first-century Jewish historian and contemporary of both Jesus and Paul, infamously asserted: "The woman, says the Law, is in all things inferior to the man."[19] And a modern expert on women's lives during the time period of the apostolic witness, Dr. David Scholer, sums up how women were perceived in Jewish and the larger Greco-Roman society: "In very general terms Jesus lived in social-cultural contexts in which the male view of women was usually negative and the place of women was understood to be limited for the most part to the domestic roles of wife and mother."[20]

Therefore, the description of Jesus's posse as a dozen mistake-prone men *and* three chicks was a shocking concept.[21] By allowing them to be an integral part of His public ministry, Jesus challenged a centuries-old paradigm of women being subjugated as second-class citizens. Contrary to culture, Jesus's inner circle proves He considered women to be valuable; He treated them as trusted companions and worthy ambassadors of the Gospel. And they returned the favor because the phrase "many others" and the pronoun "who" are both feminine in the original Greek manuscripts of Luke,[22] which means Mary, Joanna, and Susanna had gal pals who supported Jesus's ministry as well. Picture a first-century book club filled with chicks who wrote checks! Which means Jesus didn't view women as weak and dependent. He didn't patronize them when they pulled out their purses and say, "Put that away. You girls save your money because there's an awesome mall in the next village!" Instead, He humbly allowed them to invest in His life's work. He treated them with dignity.

And they weren't just baking cookies and casseroles when they weren't writing checks, either. In fact, Joanna (a woman of position and means) was probably the head of His security detail because her spouse, Chuza, was Herod Antipas's right-hand man. Remember, Herod Antipas is the same womanizer who had John the Baptist murdered for calling him out on sexual immorality (Mark 6:14–29). Plus, his father, Herod the Great, was the megalomaniac who schemed to have Jesus killed when He was a baby (Matt. 2:16). Which means Joanna's missionary work with the Messiah was going on right under the enemy's nose. Can you imagine how interesting Joanna and Chuza's pillow talk was? And can you imagine how much courage it took to maintain an alliance with Jesus (all the way to the cross, mind you) when her husband's boss—a very powerful and jealous narcissist—was His archrival? It's amazing to think about: that much extremely important intel flowing through the vessel of a *woman*. (Not to mention a *married* woman, who would have undoubtedly endured a lot of societal suspicion for following, learning from, serving, and publicly supporting a man like Jesus without her husband around!)

Then there's Mary Magdalene, whom Luke describes as being afflicted by seven demons (she's the only person healed from demon possession in the four Gospels whose exact number of demons is specified) before she encountered Jesus and was healed. And remember the number seven illustrates completion in biblical literature, so it implies that she was *completely* oppressed by the enemy. (Please forgive me the intentional grammatical error of not capitalizing that lying lizard's name, even though "enemy" or "satan" are technically proper pronouns!) Yet John's Gospel describes *this* very Mary as the very first person to see the risen Messiah. Which surely caused more than a few to cry, "FOUL!"

Most folks probably raised their eyebrows and wondered: "Is she really the *best* spokesperson for the resurrection of our Lord Jesus?" In fact, based on their initial dismissal of her claim (Mark 16:11; Luke 24:10–11), even the disciples, who'd known Mary for years, seemed to think the cause of Christ would be far better off with a more credible eyewitness to Easter.

I've heard the resurrection described as "the fulcrum of the Christian faith." In other words, our entire belief system hinges on Easter—on the fact that our Savior didn't stay dead. And don't forget, our Creator-Redeemer is a God of details; He put stripes on zebras and gave cells their nucleus—so you can bet *everything* about that first Easter week was preordained, from the placement of the cross to the borrowed tomb. Therefore, don't you think it's incredibly cool that God chose Mary Magdalene—not just a *woman*, but one who'd been totally marginalized—for what is arguably the most important job in human history? To be the very first person to testify that Jesus has indeed come back to life!

- **READ ROMANS 8:12-17.** Note that in the beginning of the passage, the word *brothers* in the original language doesn't refer to gender in this particular context, but instead to all fellow believers—to brothers *and* sisters. Knowing this, how does your understanding and application of this text change?

- **READ NUMBERS 27:1-11.** How does this passage help prove that, contrary to some modern assumptions, our Creator-Redeemer was *not* a misogynist?

Day 28

JESUS'S CROSS IS TRANSFORMATIVE

When the hour came, he reclined at the table, and the apostles with him. Then he said to them, "I have fervently desired to eat this Passover with you before I suffer. For I tell you, I will not eat it again until it is fulfilled in the kingdom of God." Then he took a cup, and after giving thanks, he said, "Take this and share it among yourselves. For I tell you, from now on I will not drink of the fruit of the vine until the kingdom of God comes."

And he took bread, gave thanks, broke it, gave it to them, and said, "This is my body, which is given for you. Do this in remembrance of me."

In the same way he also took the cup after supper and said, "This cup is the new covenant in my blood, which is poured out for you. But look, the hand of the one betraying me is at the table with me. For the Son of Man will go away as it has been determined, but woe to that man by whom he is betrayed!"

So they began to argue among themselves which of them it could be who was going to do it.

Then a dispute also arose among them about who should be considered the greatest. LUKE 22:14–24, EMPHASIS MINE

DESPITE THE SERENITY DEPICTED in Renaissance paintings, that Last Supper held in an "upper room" (those two words in the New Testament come from the single Greek word *kataluma,* which was typically a guest room people rented out—similar to a modern-day Airbnb), where Jesus shared a Passover meal with His handpicked posse of disciples, was anything but peaceful. I can totally imagine breadsticks flying as that motley crew started fussing! However, I can't begin to imagine how disheartened Jesus was when what was supposed to be a holy and grateful observance of how God had spared the Jewish people from death during the Egyptian captivity digressed into a raucous sort of reality television show.

Instead of the supper being marked by brotherly cohesion, it was marked by prideful division—by an ugly argument over who'd have top billing in Glory. These twelve guys—who'd spent *three years* with Jesus—were still so consumed by their own agendas that they completely missed that the Old Testament prophecies about the Messiah's sacrificial death were about to be fulfilled. It would've made sense if Jesus had chosen to fry them all into a grease spot of oblivion and chucked the whole "redemption of humanity" plan! Instead, John tells us that He stooped down, picked up a wet towel, and began to wash their nasty feet (John 13:1–17). After this, He walked to the Mount of Olives where Judas's betrayal—which He knows is a precursor to His crucifixion—was going to take place.

Fifty days later, the disciples had a Pentecost dinner in another upper room, only this time the meal didn't morph into a melee:

> *When they arrived, they went to the room upstairs where they were staying*: Peter, John, James, Andrew, Philip, Thomas, Bartholomew, Matthew, James the son of Alphaeus, Simon the Zealot, and Judas *the* son of James. *They all were continually united in prayer,* along with the women, including Mary the mother of Jesus, and his brothers. (Acts 1:13–14, emphasis mine)

Less than two months had passed since their disastrous Passover dinner and the posture of these eleven men has been completely transformed from divided and prideful to devoted and prayerful. They're no longer simply consumers of the Gospel, but have matured into carriers of the Gospel. We know this because the rest of the story tells us that, for example, all but John would ultimately give their lives for the sake of Christ, and as for Peter, legend has it that he humbly asked to be crucified upside down rather than right side up because he knew he wasn't worthy to adopt the posture of Jesus in death. What happened in seven weeks that left such a life-changing mark on these men?

The cross and the resurrection happened.

Peter experienced radical restoration less than two weeks after he threw Jesus under the bus. Thomas was invited to touch the wounds in Jesus's wrists where Roman soldiers had driven metal stakes on which the weight of His body would hang. All of them got to see Jesus in the flesh, risen, after He had died. They finally understood in part what their Savior had been prophesying all along: I love you so much, I'd rather die (and then conquer death) than live without you.

The difference between performance and devotion is rarely defined by outward behavior. When I was shackled with shame in my twenties and thirties, I still read my Bible and prayed and tried not to say bad words in traffic. Outwardly, a Pharisee and a devotee can look similar. But when your heart becomes more cognizant of what took place on (and after!) that old, rugged cross, *everything* changes.

- **AUTHOR BARBARA JOHNSON** wrote: "We're Easter people living in a Good Friday world."[23] How would you restate that in your own words?

- **IT'S BEEN SAID** that Protestants "take Jesus off the cross too quickly" and don't spend enough time pondering what He went through on our behalf. Do you agree or disagree? How might *considering* the *crucifixion* help you become a "carrier" of the Gospel more so than a "consumer"?

Day 29

JESUS IS THE PRINCE OF PEACE

*"Let not your hearts be troubled. Believe in God; believe also in me. In my
Father's house are many rooms. If it were not so, would I have told you that I go
to prepare a place for you? And if I go and prepare a place for you, I will come
again and will take you to myself, that where I am you may be also."*

*"Peace I leave with you; my peace I give to you. Not as the world gives do I give to you.
Let not your hearts be troubled, neither let them be afraid."* JOHN 14:1–3; 27 ESV

THE DAY I WROTE today's devotional entry was the day after Christmas, and
you know what I remember most about it? Waking up early to the most serene
sound of silence. It took me a moment to adjust because even though we live
on a five-acre "farmette" way out in the country, there's almost always some
kind of rural alarm clock like the distant crowing of a neighbor's rooster or the
cows of another neighbor mooing or birds singing in the cedar trees outside
my bedroom or our oldest, sweetest dog Cookie begging to be let out because
her bladder's even weaker than mine! But this morning there was nothing but
quiet, so I got out of bed and before I even opened the curtains, I realized, "Oh,
it must be snowing." And sure enough, when I looked outside, those Tennessee
hills our log home is nestled among were wearing robes of white.

I stood at the window for a long time soaking in the beauty of the landscape.
All of the severe browns of winter, the leafless trees and dead grass, and even
the damage caused by the ice storm we had on Christmas Eve were gently cam-
ouflaged by snow. The soundscape was lovely too, because the blanket of snow
muffled harsh sounds (like the rumble of a lonely salt truck on the highway
down below) and seemed to accentuate softer noises (like the dripping icicles
on the deck or the soft snoring of my daughter, who had been sleeping in my
room that Advent season because what I thought was a two-day tiling project in
her bathroom had stretched into a multi-week adventure complete with a toilet
in the middle of her bedroom!).

Of course, I didn't mind sharing my bed with Missy for a few weeks—despite
her kicking like a mule, hogging the blankets, and systematically scooching me
to the edge of the bed throughout the night until I'm clinging to the outside

seam of the mattress to keep from being dumped on the cold floor! Who knew that an unconscious sixth grader could so effectively and entirely command every inch of a king-sized bed? Yet as incongruous as it may sound, enjoying a bit less sleep due to nocturnal shoving for those sweet few weeks was as quieting internally as the fresh snow was externally. Because I never dreamed my life could be that peaceful, much less have the faith to pray that it would be so.

I spent decades running as hard and fast as I could in the hopes of attaining God's pleasure and other people's approval. I was so worried about not being *enough* that I sacrificed much of my security and contentment on the altar of anxiety. Even after I matured to the point of cognitively understanding that God's love isn't accelerated by my productivity—that my worth isn't equivalent to my work—my heart still wasn't quiet. It had danced to the deafening tune of "I don't deserve" for so long that it took a while for the divine melody of serenity to become emotionally audible, for our Savior's generous promise of a life rich in peace and poor in trouble to become my natural rhythm.

So, as you can imagine, it felt somewhat surreal to sit there on that snowy, late-December morning, sipping a hot cup of coffee beside a cozy fire in the company of two sleeping dogs and one sleeping daughter, flushed with fresh gratitude. I didn't have the strength to lug my heavy, hypervigilant heart to a place of tranquility, but Jesus did.

As you walk into this day, remember: peace may not come naturally to you, but it is possible. Its Prince went to great lengths to bring it to you, so perhaps take a moment to simply pause long enough to let it surprise you. It is there for you to sit and savor for a while, no matter what circumstances or window you find yourself looking through.

- **IF YOU HAD** to paint a picture or scene of peace, what would it look like?

- **READ JOHN 14:1** and 1 Peter 5:7. What is your "loudest" trouble/worry this season?

- **TAKE A MOMENT** to reflect on a relationship and/or situation God has redeemed in your life that you're especially grateful for. Does intentional gratitude help quiet your worry and restore some measure of peacefulness?

Day 30
JESUS IS IN THE OLD TESTAMENT TOO

Now that same day two of them were on their way to a village called Emmaus, which was about seven miles from Jerusalem. Together they were discussing everything that had taken place. And while they were discussing and arguing, Jesus himself came near and began to walk along with them. But they were prevented from recognizing him. Then he asked them, "What is this dispute that you're having with each other as you are walking?" And they stopped walking and looked discouraged.

The one named Cleopas answered him, "Are you the only visitor in Jerusalem who doesn't know the things that happened there in these days?"

"What things?" he asked them.

So they said to him, "The things concerning Jesus of Nazareth, who was a prophet powerful in action and speech before God and all the people, and how our chief priests and leaders handed him over to be sentenced to death, and they crucified him. But we were hoping that he was the one who was about to redeem Israel. Besides all this, it's the third day since these things happened. Moreover, some women from our group astounded us. They arrived early at the tomb, and when they didn't find his body, they came and reported that they had seen a vision of angels who said he was alive. Some of those who were with us went to the tomb and found it just as the women had said, but they didn't see him."

He said to them, "How foolish you are, and how slow to believe all that the prophets have spoken! Wasn't it necessary for the Messiah to suffer these things and enter into his glory?" <u>*Then beginning with Moses and all the Prophets, he interpreted for them the things concerning himself in all the Scriptures.*</u> LUKE 24:13–27, EMPHASIS MINE

I WAS LISTENING TO a podcast recently and heard a lovely woman I used to learn from describe her personal Christian deconstruction narrative and how she no longer considers the Bible something that can be read with certainty. She encouraged listeners who remained inclined to read the Bible to do so purely as an inspirational endeavor and emphatically declared that if one wants to know what Jesus taught, they should focus solely on the red letters in the four New Testament Gospel accounts because that's the *only* time He shows up in the story! Sadly, her opinion has become all too common in modern culture with more and more self-proclaimed experts clamoring to deconstruct the authority of God's Word and the divine nature of Christ Himself.

I'm not a formally trained apologist—my doctorate is in Spiritual Formation—and I take no pleasure in doctrinal fisticuffs (it took years of therapy for me to learn how to healthily engage in conflict, but I still tend to avoid it with more gusto that I do steamed kale or unemployed blind dates who live in their mother's basements!). But I can't help noticing the gaping holes in this flawed logic. Besides a plethora of passages illustrating the preexistent, self-sustaining, trinitarian nature of God the Father, God the Son, and God the Holy Spirit (including but not limited to: Gen. 1:26–27, 3:22; Isa. 6:8; Job 19:25–27; Matt. 3:16–17; Luke 3:21–22; John 1:1–18, 29–34; Eph. 4:4–6; Col. 1:15–17; Heb. 1:3; and 1 Pet. 1:1–2), we've got almost two thousand years of theological scaffolding built by saints and scholars who devoted their entire lives to seeking God through His enscripturated revelation and serving others for His namesake. Therefore, I think the bulwark of biblical Christianity can withstand the softballs lobbed by social media influencers posing as purveyors of truth!

Plus, we've got the Emmaus Road encounter in Luke 24—which I like to call *Jesus's own Christological explanation of Himself as seen in the Old Testament!*

These two guys are walking home to the suburbs of Emmaus after experiencing the very first Passion week in the big city of Jerusalem. They're walking along with their heads down, kicking at pebbles on the dirt road, because they're completely flummoxed by what they just witnessed. They assumed Jesus was going to be the king who would liberate them out from under the oppressive authority of Rome, but instead He was killed on a cross less than a week after Jerusalem held a parade in His honor. It just didn't make sense to them.

But then Jesus—whom they didn't yet recognize—sidles up next to this despairing duo and effectively asks: "Why the long faces, guys?" After giving each other a sideways glance that said "How does this yahoo *not know* what just happened in Jerusalem?" they go on to explain (likely with some impatience or even condescension) the events that had just taken place from Palm Sunday to Easter.

After patiently listening to their sad saga, our Savior basically replies (and I picture Him with a hint of a smile here): "Don't you guys remember? We studied this in Torah 101. The prophets told us this would happen!" And starting with a lesson from the Pentateuch, He continues all the way through to the end of the Hebrew Bible, interpreting for them the things concerning Himself *in all the Scriptures.* In other words, Jesus takes these two discouraged dudes on a comprehensive Old Testament tour and makes it clear: *all of this is about Me!*

Don't limit yourself to just the red letters, y'all—every single letter of this divine love story we call the Bible is saturated with the promise of redemption! Frankly, I think if you look hard enough, you can find the compassionate countenance of Jesus on each page, no matter which Testament!

- **"SHADOW AND SUBSTANCE"** is a term that describes how we can see the promise of redemption in the Old Testament and the fulfillment of redemption in the New Testament. Besides an obvious love story like Hosea (whose name is the Hebrew equivalent of the Greek name Jesus!) and Gomer, can you name a few other Old Testament stories that are filled with the "shadow" of Jesus?

- **READ JOB 19:25-27.** Now look up the Hebrew word for Redeemer, which is *Go'el*. How does Job's prophetic assertion point to Jesus?

- **CONSIDER JOHN 5:46,** 8:52–58, and 12:39–41. Also consider 1 Peter 1:10–12. What do these passages teach about Christ's presence in the Old Testament, and the knowledge that Hebrew patriarchs and prophets had about Him?

Day 31

JESUS IS THE CLEAR FULFILLMENT OF
OLD TESTAMENT PROPHECY

MY NAME IS LISA and I'm a recovering skeptic. My distrust began when I was a little girl and was molested by a phony of a deacon who did more damage in the dark than he could ever redeem by teaching Sunday school. Then, after finding out as a teenager that one of the pastors of the church I attended with my dad (my parents were divorced so I was involved in several different churches while growing up) had a long-running affair that was covered up by elders to mitigate potential damage to the church's reputation and bank account, I became increasingly wary. I didn't wonder so much about God's character, but I formed deep suspicions about how much honesty existed within His church. By the time I was in college, I'd digressed to the point that if I couldn't find historical and pragmatic "proof" with regard to something in the spiritual realm, I didn't believe it. Which, of course, doesn't bode very well for a person of *faith*.

Despite my aversion to dishonesty, I was rarely forthcoming about my own lack of trust. Since the few folks I'd shared my struggles with reacted with disapproval and one insisted on slathering me with oil and hollering to help rid me of such "evil thoughts," I learned to keep my concerns largely to myself. My nose was always up (pun intended) when it came to sniffing out religious charlatans attempting to fleece unsuspecting flocks, but I stopped talking about it. I joined my friends in praying for miracles and supernatural stuff like that, but only with eyes wide-open and always on the lookout for emotive shenanigans masquerading as the Holy Spirit!

You can probably imagine my reticence when I was about thirty and a friend of a friend named Rita told me that God had spoken to her in a dream about me having a daughter. It was all I could do not to inquire about whether she'd eaten extremely spicy food prior to having that oh-so-personal dream about me! When she explained further that I would become a mother through adoption, I was outwardly polite but inwardly dismissive. By then I'd all but forgotten how my best friend in high school, Cindy, and I had studied the theme of adoption while leading a Bible study together and made a pact to each adopt children when we got older. Rita calmly and respectfully shared several more details about my impending parenthood and future daughter that she sensed were from the Lord, and while I don't remember how I responded verbatim, my emotional eye roll could've caused a tidal wave. To her great credit she responded with much more grace twenty years later, after I brought Missy home from Haiti, and had the humbling joy of telling her that every single detail of her dream had come true!

Before we go any further, I do want to add a brief disclaimer because a dream or vision is much more subjective than enscripturated prophecies (which just means the ones that became actual Scripture, like the examples listed below!) because they can be misinterpreted or manipulated by whoever supposedly had it, and not all "dreamers" are as spiritually mature as my friend Rita. For instance, if I told you God gave me a dream about my future nuptials with Brad Pitt, that *would* be the result of too much spicy food and not a divine nudge! I'm not advocating that we kick common sense to the curb and, of course, we must always pray for discernment from the Holy Spirit about such things. However, for those of you who, like me, tend to be wary about *anything* you can't nail down with facts, here are just a few biblical prophecies about Jesus that should add some fuel to your belief tank:

- Isaiah 7:14 prophesies that the Messiah will be born to a virgin, which clearly happens in Luke 1:26–35.

- Micah 5:2–5 prophesies that the Messiah will be born in Bethlehem of Judea, which clearly happens in Luke 2:4–7.

- Psalm 72:10–11 prophesies that kings will bring the Messiah gifts and render Him tribute, which clearly happens in Matthew 2:7–11.

- Second Samuel 7:12–13 prophesies that the Messiah will be a king, from the line of David, which is clearly recorded in Acts 13:22–23.

- Psalm 78:2 prophesies that the Messiah will speak in parables, which is recorded throughout the Gospels.

- Isaiah 40 and Malachi 3 prophesy that someone will prepare the way for the Messiah, which clearly happens through the person and ministry of John the Baptist, as recorded in all four Gospel accounts (i.e., John 1:21–28).

- Zechariah 9:9 prophesies that the Messiah will enter Jerusalem on a colt, which clearly happened during the triumphal entry in John 12:13–15.

- Zechariah 11:12 prophesies that the Messiah would be sold for thirty pieces of silver, which clearly happens through Judas Iscariot's betrayal (Matt. 26:14–15).

- Zechariah 11:13 prophesies that those thirty pieces of silver would then be used to buy a potter's field, which clearly happens after Judas committed suicide (Matt. 27:3–7).

- Numbers 9:9–12 prophesies that the Messiah will be a Passover sacrifice but not a bone in His body would be broken, both of which are recorded in the crucifixion narrative (John 19:31–33).

- Deuteronomy 21:22–23 prophesies that the Messiah would be hung on a tree as a curse for us, which apostle Paul recounts in Galatians 3:13–14.

- Psalm 22:15 prophesies that the Messiah would be thirsty during His execution and Psalm 69:20–21 prophecies that He would be given sour wine, both of which are recorded in the crucifixion narrative (John 19:28; Luke 23:36).

- Micah 5:1 prophesies that the Messiah would be struck on the cheek, which is recorded in the crucifixion narrative (Matt. 27:30).

- Daniel 7:13–14 prophesies that the Messiah will not stay dead but will have an everlasting dominion and kingdom that can't be destroyed, which is explained by apostle Paul in Romans 6 and 2 Corinthians 5, and by John the apostle throughout the entire book of Revelation!

Now may I encourage you to set your skepticism on a shelf some warm evening soon and go outside and lie in the grass (you might need to go to the roof for this exercise in putting practicality back into healthy alignment if you're an urbanite) and look up at the stars for a long moment or two? Or watch ocean waves ebb and flow. Or hold a baby. Or watch puppies play. Or behold lightning in the distance. Or watch the sun set. Or watch the sun rise. Wariness is kind of like salt, y'all—a little bit makes some things taste better (and can keep you from getting run over in the Walmart parking lot!), but a whole lot will ruin the entire meal.

- **WHAT MEMORIES IN** your spiritual history have tempted you to approach the world with wariness?

- **IT'S CLEAR FROM** these passages that God kept His promises about Christ's coming, even if it took thousands of years. And if God keeps His promises about something as massively important as *Christ*, He will certainly keep His promises to you in the details of your daily life. In what specific ways or seasons has God kept His promises to you over the years?

- **THESE PASSAGES HELP** us see that Christ is the fulfillment of all that was foretold in the Old Testament—of everything His people needed. What things do you run to for fulfillment of everything you need? In what ways is Christ a better fulfillment than those things?

Day 32

JESUS IS PREOCCUPIED
WITH OUR WELL-BEING

I pray for them. I am not praying for the world, but for those you have given me, for they are yours. All I have is yours, and all you have is mine. And glory has come to me through them. I will remain in the world no longer, but they are still in the world, and I am coming to you. <u>Holy Father, protect them</u> by the power of your name, the name you gave me, so that they may be one as we are one. <u>While I was with them, I protected them and kept them safe</u> by that name you gave me. None has been lost except the one doomed to destruction so that Scripture would be fulfilled. JOHN 17:9–12 NIV, EMPHASIS MINE

I HAD LOTS OF professional counseling as well as peer counseling (with other adoptive parents) before bringing Missy home from Haiti and one of the common rules of thumb was to be careful about overstimulation while she was settling in. I was warned specifically about making too much of a fuss during our first major holidays together. Both the counselor and other experienced adoptive parents said too many gifts or celebratory revelry would likely overwhelm her and possibly even cause some type of trauma response after the extreme scarcity she was used to in Haiti.

Remarkable restraint is the only way to describe me during our first Christmas together. Especially since I'd initially planned a Clark Griswold, enough-outdoor-lights-to-attract-small-planes and enough-gifts-to-fill-the-living-room-floor kind of affair! I reluctantly scrapped the elaborate light display and scaled *way* back on purchases (even though it about killed me to cancel the order for the pony with pink satin ribbons braided in her mane and tail!). Of course, my friends and counselor were right. Missy was pleased with her small assortment of modest gifts, especially a little battery-operated train. We spent most of our first Christmas Day together peacefully sprawled out in the living room watching that tiny, three-car train go round and round and round. It was a lovely, low-key affair.

However, the following Christmas—and every Christmas since—I decided not to leave well enough alone. I've waited to be a parent for decades doggone it, which means I've *earned the right* to stay up all night on Christmas Eve putting together giant, complex toys and things to ride that come with real motors and instructions printed in foreign languages! And I'm happy to report that despite the multiple broken fingernails, bruises, and gashes (no kidding, I can show you the scars) I've sustained while putting together bikes and four-wheelers and scooters and Segways (yep, but it was a small, noncommercial one) through the years, Missy has never been overwhelmed (mind you, she's been underwhelmed a time or two by "educational" toys), much less injured. Because even though I tend to transform into Santa-on-steroids for a few weeks each December, my inner protective-mama always wins out to the point that I have double safety mechanisms installed on my daughter's various assortment of go-go gadgets and her helmet is sturdy enough to withstand an elephant pirouetting on top of it. I might get a little carried away at Christmas, but I'm not about to let my kid get *hurt*!

As preoccupied as I am with Missy's well-being, isn't it comforting to know that Jesus is infinitely more so with ours? In our Savior's High Priestly prayer, which He uttered soon after Judas's betrayal (the only one "doomed to destruction") and right before His arrest in the garden of Gethsemane, He pleads with God the Father for *our* safety. And don't miss the poignancy of the context here, y'all; it's Thursday night of Passion Week . . . *Good Friday Eve*. Which means His tortuous death on the cross is right around the corner. And because Jesus is omniscient (remember He's of the exact nature and substance of God), He *knows* His murder is imminent. He *knows* He's not safe. Yet instead of pleading with Yahweh for His own well-being, He pleads for ours!

And the specific words He uses when He prays for our salvific protection add a big exclamation point to our super-secure position as those guarded by the King of all kings: "While I was with them, I *protected* them and *kept* them safe" (John 17:12a, emphasis mine). Because while the verbs "protected" (*phulassō* in the original Greek) and "kept" (*tēreō* in the original Greek) are synonymous, one is in the aorist tense, which usually denotes an action in past tense, and one is in the imperfect tense, which usually denotes an action in the present tense.[24] All that fancy, syntax footwork simply means is we are *continuously protected by* Jesus. Which is so much better than having your mom Bubble Wrap the walls of your college dorm room, which may very well be a future chapter in Missy's story!

- **ONE OF MY** favorite love songs in college was sung by an English rock band called The Police and it includes the lyrics: "Every breath you take, every move you make, every bond you break, every step you take, I'll be watching you."[25] It sounds pretty stalkerish now when I remember how passionately my nineteen-year-old boyfriend sang it, but it's a galvanizing theological truism when it comes to Jesus and us! What emotion comes to mind when you consider the fact that Jesus is watching protectively over every step you take?

- **READ 1 PETER 1:3-9.** Again, the words *kept* and *guarded* (vv. 4 and 5) might sound a tad overprotective or even possessive in our current cultural context (especially if you have a Bubble-Wrapping kind of mom!), yet they're radically promissory in the context of our relationship with Jesus. What are some other words—perhaps more comfortable/comforting to you personally—that describe the consummate and continual divine protection we get to enjoy as God's people?

- **READ JOB 1** and Psalm 119:75. In light of David's lyric, Job's story, and surely your own life experience, it's obvious that God's protection doesn't mean we'll be immune to pain and suffering. So what do you think Jesus was really asking when He pleaded for God to protect us?

Day 33

JESUS IS A RELENTLESS PURSUER

He also said, "A man had two sons. The younger of them said to his father, 'Father, give me the share of the estate I have coming to me.' So he distributed the assets to them. Not many days later, the younger son gathered together all he had and traveled to a distant country, where he squandered his estate in foolish living. After he had spent everything, a severe famine struck that country, and he had nothing. Then he went to work for one of the citizens of that country, who sent him into his fields to feed pigs. He longed to eat his fill from the pods that the pigs were eating, but no one would give him anything. When he came to his senses, he said, 'How many of my father's hired workers have more than enough food, and here I am dying of hunger! I'll get up, go to my father, and say to him, "Father, I have sinned against heaven and in your sight. I'm no longer worthy to be called your son. Make me like one of your hired workers."' So he got up and went to his father. But while the son was still a long way off, his father saw him and was filled with compassion. He ran, threw his arms around his neck, and kissed him." LUKE 15:11–20

I'VE SPENT A LOT of time volunteering at a faith-based, residential program for women recovering from addiction to drugs or alcohol in downtown Nashville. If you've ever had the privilege of spending time with recovering addicts, you know it's an amazing experience as well as a very messy, complicated, and often brutally honest one. Women who've been busted for possession with the intent to sell and have spent years in prison as a result usually don't feel the need to wear façades anymore. Frankly, I wish our congregations and small groups and Sunday school classes were as authentic as the addiction recovery community.

Anyway, as a result of my volunteer work, I've had the undeserved privilege of being invited to attend a few Alcoholics Anonymous and Narcotics Anonymous meetings. And my friend "Becky" shared a story at one of those meetings that wedged itself deeply into my heart like a redemptive splinter. (Please note: I've changed the identifying details in this true story out of respect for my friends and my pledge to keep their stories anonymous.)

As is customary at every AA or NA meeting, she began with the phrase, "Hi, my name's Becky and I'm an addict." After the rest of the group responded with a hearty, "Hi, Becky!" she began with the happy proclamation: "I was so thankful to be cleaning those tubs today, y'all!" As the rest of her testimony about how Jesus (whom she'd given her heart to as a little girl before physical and sexual abuse sent her careening toward self-destruction) had turned her life around tumbled out, I found out the day of the meeting coincided with her first day of employment at a hotel.

She explained how grateful she was for her new job as a full-time maid because she'd pounded the pavement for over a month and had turned in *one hundred and fourteen* job applications before finally landing a gig. Mind you, it wasn't her first day of *work*, but it was her first eight-hour shift with a company that pays Social Security taxes and gives its employees benefits. Her former job had been selling her body to men who sometimes handed her a twenty-dollar bill or a small rock of crack cocaine and often gave her a sexually transmitted disease or a closed fist across the face.

I don't think I'll ever forget the last thing she said at that NA meeting. She shared how earlier that day she'd stood up in the hotel bathroom she was cleaning to stretch. When she did, she caught her reflection in the mirror. Her voice caught for a second while she was describing the scene and she took a deep breath to steady herself, then she said firmly, "That's the first time since I was six- or seven-years-old that I looked in a mirror and liked what I saw." She's beginning to believe again how very much Jesus loves her. She's finally beginning to respond positively to His relentless pursuit.

Becky's personal revival reminds me of that familiar story in Luke's Gospel account. When Jesus narrated a somewhat cautionary, ultimately heartwarming tale about a rebellious young man who coerced his dad into giving him early access to his trust fund. You probably remember that prodigal went on to spend it all in some ancient Vegas—on cards and call girls—and ended up living in the equivalent of a homeless shelter. There, he finally recognized the foolish and destructive nature of his hard-partying lifestyle and decided to go back home.

He was broke, humiliated, and repentant. But on the bus ride home, he began to ponder what his dad's reaction would be to his homecoming. He assumed that, at best, he'd receive a furious lecture and be exiled to their garage apartment. At worst, he probably thought he'd face banishment from his family forever, the thought of which made him despondent. He could barely raise his head from his hands when the bus driver announced his stop. But then, as he paused to adjust his heavy backpack while descending the bus steps to keep from toppling over, he spotted his dad running across the parking lot toward him, waving his arms wildly over his head, and bellowing, "Son, son, over here!

I'm over here! Welcome home. . . . WELCOME HOME!" And that precious prodigal was stunned speechless when his father rushed up and pulled him into a prolonged bear hug.

Jesus told that beautiful story to breathe redemptive hope into the Becky who resides in some small corner of all our crooked little hearts. To reveal that His love is bigger than our rebellion. To illustrate that no matter how far we wander, we will always have a welcoming embrace to come home to. To bellow that instead of abandoning us to our sin, He will run to redeem us. His grace really is that relentless.

- **READ PSALM 23:6.** How does it affect you to find out the word *follow* in the original language actually means "to follow after," as in, *to pursue*? In other words, God's divine mercy and goodness aren't rolling along behind you like a caboose, they're chasing you like a bloodhound!

- **READ PSALM 139:7-8.** Since God is with us everywhere we go, do you think loneliness is a true reality for the believer, or a warped perception caused by unbelief? What steps could you take to increase your awareness of God's nearness?

- **ARE YOU RUNNING** from God in any area of your life? Why? How does this story help infuse you with the courage to run home to Him?

Day 34

JESUS IS THE LAST ADAM

So it is written, The first man Adam became a living being; the last Adam became a life-giving spirit. However, the spiritual is not first, but the natural, then the spiritual.

The first man was from the earth, a man of dust; the second man is from heaven. Like the man of dust, so are those who are of the dust; like the man of heaven, so are those who are of heaven. And just as we have borne the image of the man of dust, we will also bear the image of the man of heaven. 1 CORINTHIANS 15:45–49

I'VE BEEN MISTAKEN FOR three different country music artists over the years here in Nashville. One time this experience took place when I was wearing a cowboy hat on a bad hair day and a woman followed me around Pier One, determined to get a picture with me because she thought I was Terri Clark. That was the most flattering encounter—for me, not Terri's fan, who stalked off quite disappointed when I took my hat off and said, "Ma'am, I promise I'm not her." The least flattering encounter was when a man chased me down in a parking garage yelling excitedly, "Ronnie . . . hey, Ronnie!" When he breathlessly caught up to me, he sputtered, "Well shoot, you're not Ronnie Milsap!" Neither one of us knew quite what to say for a few seconds. He was disappointed that I wasn't his favorite singer, and I was even more disappointed that he'd gotten me confused with his favorite *male* singer.

But by far the most awkward mistaken identity case happened years ago when I helped lead a business leader's Bible study. Because the gathering took place in the middle of Nashville's busy downtown area, it was always tricky to find a parking spot every week. I was thrilled when a new pay lot opened up right across the street from where we met at noon on Wednesdays. Although I was a little confused when I stopped to pay the attendant and he saluted me with an enthusiastic, "Hey ho, Miss O!"

It wasn't until the following week when he winked with friendly familiarity and said something along the lines of, "I've been listening to your music a lot since I saw you last Wednesday!" that it registered to me he thought I was a musician. The third week, when I tried to politely explain that he had me confused with another person, he winked and said, "You can trust me, Miss K. T., I won't tell anyone else you're parking here!" and waved me off jauntily so he could process the payment of the person behind me. Finally, on the fourth week, I pulled out my driver's license to prove that I really wasn't K. T. Oslin—the extremely gifted, three-time Grammy winner with the huge "80's Ladies" hit song, who just so happened to be twenty years older than me!

If I could choose to be someone's doppelgänger, it would be a woman closer to my age. And I'm sure if those incredible artists got to choose their own doppelgängers, they wouldn't have chosen me because I can't carry a tune in a bucket!

When we hear or read the descriptive theological phrase, "Jesus is the Last Adam," (some passages and Bible translations also use the term "Second Adam"), it's easy to assume that awkward vernacular is suggesting our Savior was *like* Adam—perhaps a better look-alike than I was for Ronnie—but nonetheless, it sounds like the King of all kings has been confused for Eve's husband, the first human of the entire human race. But it's so much better than a case of mistaken identity, y'all!

Remember the guy who was a mean-spirited attorney who hated Christians until the Messiah zapped him blind on the road to Damascus and had a literal "come to Jesus" convo with him, after which he became a devout Christ-follower and used his brilliant intellect and transformed heart to write a big chunk of the New Testament, and in so doing to lay the foundation of Christian doctrine (Acts 9)? That's Paul, and he is the one who came up with the "Last Adam" concept. The basic summation of Paul's logic is that while "Adam was the representative head of old creation, through whom came death, Christ is the representative man of new creation, through whom comes the resurrection of the dead."[26] Or, said another way, because first Adam led the human race into sin, we are now inheritors of *death*—meaning our bodies are now all inherited from Adam in perishable form. Our fallen state and decaying bodies are inherited because we belong to Adam. But Jesus came on the scene to undo all that as a new head of humanity, and once we belong to Him, we get the opposite—we inherit *life* (supernatural, resurrected bodies that are freed from all the fallenness Adam cursed us with).[27] Paul's contrast of the first Adam (who started that whole fig-leaf-pants trend in the garden of Eden) with the Last Adam/King Jesus, goes something like this:

First Adam (the guy wearing a leaf)	Last Adam/Jesus (the One wearing a crown)
Adam was a "living being" *Note, this is Paul's way of explaining Adam is in natural or "fallen" form in his physical and spiritual self, prior to redemption or resurrection, who had to *receive* life from God because he was merely human and could not grant himself life.	Jesus is a "life-giving Spirit" (1 Cor. 15:45) *Note, this is not saying Jesus is only Spirit, as if to say He's not also a physical human. Rather, it's saying Jesus (who raised from the dead in a fully glorified body) is the physical and spiritual head who *imparts* life to his followers because He is God.[28] Paul's point is that our fallen bodies can eventually resurrect into perfect (and immortal!) physical bodies because of the life-giving Spirit of Jesus![29]
Adam brought sin and death	Jesus brings redemption and new life (1 Cor. 15:21–22)
Adam emerged up from earth's dust	Jesus came down from heaven (1 Cor. 15:47–48)

Jesus is not a divine doppelgänger or a new and improved version of the first human. And He's not some proverbial Hail Mary pass by a team who's down by six with only seconds left on the clock either. Instead, Jesus was God's perfect game plan from the very beginning. He is *"the firstborn of all creation"* (Col. 1:15 ESV, emphasis mine) through whom redemption happens. Which means He has always been and always will be humanity's only hope for salvation, resurrection, and immortality forevermore!

- **WHAT ASPECT OF** that first, fig-leaf-wearing Adam's rebellion can you empathize with? When have you attempted to "hide" from God because you were so ashamed of your bad choices?

- **LOOK UP THE** word *primogeniture*. Since most of the ancient world practiced the law of primogeniture, what do you think Paul was trying to illustrate when he described Jesus as "the firstborn of all creation" (Col. 1:15 ESV)?

- **READ ROMANS 8:16–17** and Galatians 3:29. Since Scripture defines those who've put their hope in Jesus as "coheirs" with Him, what does that entitle us to?

Day 35

JESUS IS A "GO BIG OR GO HOME" KIND OF WARRIOR

Then Jesus said to his disciples, *"If anyone wants to follow after me, let him deny himself, take up his cross, and follow me. For whoever wants to save his life will lose it, but whoever loses his life because of me will find it. For what will it benefit someone if he gains the whole world yet loses his life? Or what will anyone give in exchange for his life?* MATTHEW 16:24–26

FOR MOST OF MY adult life I've enjoyed trail running. Of course, now that I'm almost sixty, it'd be more accurate to describe what I do as wobbly-trail-gasping, but trotting up and down dirt paths that wind through the woods appeals to me much more so than the monotony of running on a suburban sidewalk or a treadmill. I'd rather hear birds chirping and my own labored breathing than car horns and squealing brakes. And I'd sure rather catch a glimpse of a timid white-tailed deer bounding through the trees than a large man trudging along in too-short shorts (a sight that has alarmed me all too often when I run in the city). Plus, trail running and hiking aren't simply workouts for me, they're practical pressure-release valves. Traipsing through God's creation causes anxiety to evacuate my heart and mind in much the same way that spraying a garden hose causes my neighbor's pesky cat to sprint away from my roses!

However, about ten years ago I experienced such an unwelcome wallop in the woods that I seriously considered moving my workout routine to a comfy couch or the shallow end of a pool! There I was, hustling happily down a path in the Natchez Trace wilderness area late one afternoon, when my foot hit a slick spot and, in an instant, I was flailing through the air instead of being pleasantly attached to the ground. I crash-landed with my arms extended in front of me in an instinctive "Superman" pose. Unfortunately, I was running so fast and the trail was so steep, that the momentum propelled me facedown on the rocky path. Even more unfortunately, my nose rammed into a sharp stone with so much force that it sliced my sniffer right up the middle like a butterflied pork chop.

It took me a few seconds to gather my wits after that ungainly face-plant because I'd knocked myself silly, but I sobered up quickly when I realized blood was spurting from my nose. I knew I didn't have time to panic or whine because I was several miles from help, so I applied pressure, held my mangled nose together with my T-shirt, and ran the last half mile to my car, praying out loud the whole time. Fortunately, I have a dear friend who's a surgeon and she met me at the ER for a hasty reattachment operation, albeit without anesthesia because she had very little time to save what viable tissue was left. For a few weeks afterwards, they weren't sure if I'd keep my nose because the damage was so significant. Thankfully, it healed up nicely and all that's left from my "trail-tastrophe" is a small, rabbit-like crease of a scar.

The point of the story is what my dear friend Paige said when she came to see me at the hospital. She said, "Lisa, you're going to have to quit saying, 'we need to leave skin on the table,' when you're teaching about how we should 'go big or go home' for the sake of the Gospel!"

When I was a kid, my favorite Bible stories were the "go big or go home" ones filled with adventure. Mom reminded me not long ago that I begged her to read about Samson's exploits so often that his chapter ultimately came loose from the binding and fell out of the big picture book she read from every night! I've often wondered what Jesus's favorite stories were when He was growing up in Nazareth. Which ones did He beg Mary or Joe to read over and over again from the Hebrew Scriptures when they were putting Him to bed? In light of the fact that the Son of God grew up to fulfill His mission by going toe-to-toe with pure evil and ultimately defeated both satan and death, my guess is He was especially fond of epic battle stories like this one involving King David and one of his "Mighty Men" (who were like the ancient version of the Special Forces) named Eleazar:

> After him, Eleazar son of Dodo son of an Ahohite was among the three warriors with David when they defied the Philistines. The men of Israel retreated in the place they had gathered for battle, *but Eleazar stood his ground and attacked the Philistines until his hand was tired and stuck to his sword.* The LORD brought about a great victory that day. Then the troops came back to him, but only to plunder the dead. (2 Sam. 23:9–10, emphasis mine)

In other words, when the rest of the Israelite army abandoned King David and hightailed it out of there because they were so intimidated by the vast numbers of the Philistine army, Eleazar stood his ground with his king—likely back-to-back—and faced an entire battalion of enemy soldiers. Then, when the vicious hand-to-hand combat was finally over, all the Philistines lay dead and only King David and Eleazar were left standing. But even then Eleazar couldn't let go of his sword because he'd fought so hard for so long that his fingers were frozen stiff around the grip!

What makes this story even more gripping (pun intended) is that this incredibly lopsided victory took place at Pas-dammin, which is the very same spot that David had killed Goliath with a slingshot when he was just a boy (1 Sam. 17:1–2; 1 Chron. 11:12–14).

Can't you just picture preteen Jesus sitting up in bed cheering when His parents read this one? I like to imagine Joseph swinging a pretend sword around Jesus's bedroom as he acted out this ancient battle! Little did His parents understand then exactly how their boy would go on to become a Warrior who eclipsed the bravery of all of the Mighty Men put together when He willingly chose to leave His skin on an old, rugged cross.

And don't forget that we're made in God's image, which means we're divinely wired and equipped to be *go big* or *go home kind* of spiritual soldiers too! Whether we're on home turf standing shoulder to shoulder with an entire community of believers or whether we're totally outmanned while duking it out with the dragon, Jesus calls us to invest everything we have in the battle for His kingdom purposes.

- **WHAT'S THE BIGGEST** fight you've ever engaged in? Was it worth it?

- **WHAT NATURAL GIFTS** has God given you to invest when it comes to fighting for kingdom purposes? Do you feel like you're using them to "go big" or "run so as to win" (1 Cor. 9:24 NABRE) for the sake of the Gospel right now? Explain.

- **READ REVELATION 3:16–17.** Where do you find yourself this season on this spiritual continuum of hot (fully invested) and cold (not invested at all)?

Day 36

JESUS IS A CAPTIVATING STORYTELLER

Jesus replied with this story: *"A man prepared a great feast and sent out many invitations. When the banquet was ready, he sent his servant to tell the guests, 'Come, the banquet is ready.' But they all began making excuses. One said, 'I have just bought a field and must inspect it. Please excuse me.' Another said, 'I have just bought five pairs of oxen, and I want to try them out. Please excuse me.' Another said, 'I just got married, so I can't come.'*

"The servant returned and told his master what they had said. His master was furious and said, 'Go quickly into the streets and alleys of the town and invite the poor, the crippled, the blind, and the lame.' After the servant had done this, he reported, 'There is still room for more.' So his master said, 'Go out into the country lanes and behind the hedges and urge anyone you find to come, so that the house will be full. For none of those I first invited will get even the smallest taste of my banquet.'" LUKE 14:16–24 NLT

ONCE UPON A TIME, I attended an event for Bible teachers with lots of warm, wise peers and one aloof, insecure little girl disguised as a grown woman. For whatever reason—and I'm sure there are many—she took an instant disliking to me. She pounced on something I mispronounced at lunch and laughed derisively about a point I made at dinner, musing out loud about what sort of seminary would allow me to graduate without knowing the basics of theology. (We found out later she hadn't graduated from college, much less attended seminary, which probably fueled her poor self-esteem.) Then she lowered the boom at breakfast, after someone else at our table complimented a recent Bible study I'd written, when she declared with dripping condescension, "Well, I wouldn't call Lisa a *Bible teacher*, she's more of a *storyteller.*"

And to tell you the truth, for years I secretly believed her snarky sentiment, so I tried to mute my natural storytelling tendencies and communicate more like a "legitimate" academic. I wrote Greek and Hebrew words on the board during the classes I taught at church. I made graphs to analyze the chiastic structure of complex passages. And I always made sure to cite lots of long-dead theologians like Blaise Pascal, John Calvin, Charles Spurgeon, and G. K. Chesterton. But no matter how many pastel sweater sets I wore or how often I perched my reading glasses on top of my head, I couldn't keep up the charade and ended up feeling like a fraud—like a square peg in the round hole of biblical exegesis. (Don't get me wrong, I love to nerd out about academic concepts with my fellow theology enthusiasts, and I love learning the intricacies of Greek and Hebrew, but a jovial spirit and a love for stories is another part of myself I just can't stifle!)

I don't think I exhaled as a Gospel-slinger until a world-renowned scholar pulled me aside in our doctoral program at Denver Seminary and said with a twinkle in his eye, "Lisa, you need to remember that Jesus was a storyteller and stop trying to return the gift God has given you to communicate biblical truths in a colorful and memorable way." When he pronounced the four syllables of *storyteller* as a joyful arpeggio—like it was something wonderful instead of a plantar wart—I felt something in my heart shift with the revelation: *Jesus . . . was a storyteller.*

Although Jesus was omniscient, He wasn't obnoxious. He didn't hold Himself at arm's length. He didn't expound on Torah with elite, proprietary language that only other Smarty-McTarties could comprehend. He regularly rubbed shoulders with the *'Am Ha'arez*, which is the Hebrew term for "people of the land." In good, old American Southern vernacular, we'd call them *salt of the earth kinda folks.* And during the first century, most of those regular folks couldn't read, much less pronounce multisyllabic theological terms. So Jesus taught them spiritual concepts with imaginative language and metaphors they could understand. Almost half of His preaching repertoire was in parabolic form, which is just a fancy term for *story.*

And while the miraculous grace of the Gospel can usually be discerned in His symbolism, such as in the parable of the prodigal son, our Savior's stories were not simple nor geared toward simpletons (many of them were shared with snooty experts in the Law, mind you!). In fact, Jesus told His disciples they were *meant* to be controversial—to conceal and reveal (Matt. 13:10–17 and Mark 4:11–12)! Frankly, by relegating the biblical parables to children's Sunday school or VBS curriculums, we're missing out on some radically redemptive truths tucked behind the translucent veils of allegory.

For instance, in the parable of the great supper in Luke 14, where God's generosity (leaders, kings, landowners, or fathers in these stories almost always represent God) wasn't hindered by the rejection of those in power and was instead lavished on the missed and the marginalized, Jesus was pushing back against that era's cruel cultural bias, which catered to the elite while castigating the poor. And His social critique gets even sharper when you consider that

Jesus told this particular story after watching some hoity-toity guests jostle each other in order to nab the best seats at a fancy dinner party (v. 7)!

In short, our Savior's stories were kind of like the Superbowl or the World Cup wherein tens of thousands of people gather in a stadium to cheer for a sport, but then dramatically divide over what they want the outcome of the game to be. The parables created rabid fans *and* rude haters. They brought seekers and believers closer to Jesus, as well as illuminated their understanding about the kingdom of God, while at the same time sending His enemies stomping away in the opposite direction yammering on about how Yeshua's stories either offended them or did not make sense. Although His audiences were divided, what they were *not,* is distracted. Because He was truly captivating in the way He communicated!

- **HOW WOULD YOU** explain the Gospel of Jesus Christ to a kindergartner in the form of a fairy tale?

- **READ MARK 4:26–29.** What do you think this story reveals about God's kingdom purposes ("divine vegetation," as I like to call it) being dependent upon our labor? This petite parable illustrates why it's more biblically defensible to say, "I get to volunteer at church" than "I have to volunteer at church." In other words, it's a guilt-buster!

- **READ MARK 12:1–12.** What do you think this story reveals about God's patience with the wicked? And how can it be theologically congruent with 2 Peter 3:8–9?

Day 37
JESUS STOOPED SHOCKINGLY LOW TO LIFT US UP

Before the Passover Festival, Jesus knew that his hour had come to depart from this world to the Father. Having loved his own who were in the world, he loved them to the end.

Now when it was time for supper, the devil had already put it into the heart of Judas, Simon Iscariot's son, to betray him. Jesus knew that the Father had given everything into his hands, that he had come from God, and that he was going back to God. So he got up from supper, laid aside his outer clothing, took a towel, and tied it around himself. Next, he poured water into a basin and began to wash his disciples' feet and to dry them with the towel tied around him.

When Jesus had washed their feet and put on his outer clothing, he reclined again and said to them, "Do you know what I have done for you? You call me Teacher and Lord—and you are speaking rightly, since that is what I am. So if I, your Lord and Teacher, have washed your feet, you also ought to wash one another's feet. For I have given you an example, that you also should do just as I have done for you. JOHN 13:1–5, 12–15

I'M PRETTY OLD-FASHIONED ABOUT basic civility and treating others with respect, so the current entitled climate of modern culture is driving me a bit bonkers. Never before have I seen so much narcissistic vitriol passed off as "virtue" as I've observed in the past year or two. All you have to do is scroll through social media for a few minutes and it becomes apparent that humility and sacrifice are *not* trending! But then the way of this world has never been the way of Christ, has it? Which Paul reminds us of this in his first letter to the Corinthians: "The message of the cross is foolish to those who are headed for destruction! But *we who are being saved* know it is the very power of God" (1 Cor. 1:18 NLT, emphasis mine).

And at the risk of stepping on your toes instead of pampering them like Jesus did, "we who are being saved" are not immune to egocentrism and self-indulgence. Which probably would've been apparent if someone had polled church members to ascertain how much toilet paper we hoarded during those first few months of COVID-19! It's easy to post humblebrags online about how "love wins," but it's a whole other thing to live a life bent in the radical position of God and others-oriented service—to emulate our Savior's posture when He gave His disciples that Passover pedicure. Because, of course, the point of this passage isn't about hygiene.

Dr. D. A. Carson (yet another brilliant theologian I have a platonic crush on) explains that the central theme of Jesus's behavior and message here in John 13:1–15 isn't about the rite of foot washing (which only occurs one other time in Scripture, in 1 Timothy 5:10); rather, it's about Christ modeling humility and helpfulness.[30] In other words, the largess of God's love for us is best expressed in the context of community, through humble acts of kindness and service to each other.

And the final convicting kicker of this narrative is that during this period of ancient history, the task of foot washing was normally only performed by the lowliest of servants.

Sadly, I think far too many spiritual leaders still consider humility beneath them. It would surely behoove all of us to remember that humility comes from the Latin word *humus*, which refers to the earth or ground; therefore, becoming more honest about our own dirt could enable us to get closer to the ground as we seek to live Jesus-shaped lives.

I hope to remain forever gobsmacked by the fact that King Jesus left His throne in Glory, knowing it meant He'd not only be picking up a towel to wash the filthy feet of folks like me, but ultimately hoisting a cross on His bloody back to wash all our hearts clean from sin. And I pray the resulting gratitude will compel me to stoop increasingly lower as I lean more fully into His mercy.

- **THE WORD *EXAMPLE*** in John 13:15 comes from the original Greek word *hypodeigma*, which can also be translated "pattern." What Christ-follower in your life has a pattern of humility? In what ways could you follow their lead in the coming weeks?

- **READ MARK 10:45.** How would you distill Jesus's statement about His purpose here into a modern-day mission statement?

- **READ MATTHEW 20:25–28.** What behaviors would you have to change in order to passionately align your heart with Jesus's teaching here? What situations do you tend to be "first" in? What would it mean for you to be "last" or "low" in those same scenarios?

Day 38

JESUS DOESN'T DISTANCE
HIMSELF FROM OUR DISTRESS

Then a man with leprosy came to him and, on his knees, begged him, "If you are willing, you can make me clean." <u>Moved with compassion, Jesus reached out his hand and touched him.</u> "I am willing," he told him. "Be made clean." Immediately the leprosy left him, and he was made clean. MARK 1:40–42, EMPHASIS MINE

TWO YEARS AGO, I was rushed to the hospital with a life-threatening case of COVID that had eviscerated my lungs and wreaked havoc on the rest of my respiratory and immune systems. I'm typically a tough cookie when it comes to sickness or physical pain and don't like to complain or inconvenience others by asking for Gatorade or saltines, much less an intravenous drip. I'd much rather take a couple of Tylenol and retreat to my bedroom for a day or two like a prideful old bear in brief hibernation. But when I found myself barely able to breathe after a couple days of trying to "kick" the Delta variant of COVID-19 (which I didn't yet know I had) with rest and orange juice, I submitted to a hospital stay because I didn't really have a choice.

I was in and out of consciousness the first forty-eight hours, so it took a moment to get my bearings when a new night nurse announced he was there to check my oxygen levels. I didn't respond right away, partly because I barely had enough breath to speak, but mostly because he was wearing what looked to be an oversized bee-keeping ensemble, complete with a squarish helmet, so I thought I might be hallucinating from the meds or lack of oxygen! All the other nurses who'd bravely and compassionately taken care of me up to that point had worn protective gowns, gloves, and face shields, but none had worn homemade hazmat suits. Therefore, it took me a few flabbergasted seconds to recognize that the distorted voice coming through his glass face panel belonged to a real person who was only walking like a mummy because of the restrictive nature of the creative gear he'd chosen to barricade himself behind to keep from catching that awful and oh-so-contagious virus.

When it hit me that it was indeed a real person asking me, "Is there anything else I can do for you?" I emphatically shook my head from side to side and mouthed "No, thank you!" because I was afraid he might accidentally press the wrong button with his huge, padded gloves and turn off the machine that was steadily pumping air into my deflated lungs. Deep loneliness settled in as I watched the door close silently behind him, because I knew I had at least four more hours of gasping alone in the dark before I'd have the chance to engage with another human being. And while I didn't blame him at all for sealing himself off, I could only hope the morning nurse would be willing to touch me and maybe share a story or two.

Leprosy is not only the oldest disease in biblical history, it's considered to be one of the most contagious. The precious image-bearers who had the misfortune of catching leprosy faced crippling social stigma. According to Levitical law, they had to walk around in ripped clothes and unkempt hair, yelling, "Unclean, unclean!" whenever they were in public places so no one would engage with them and become contaminated as a result[31] (Lev. 13:45). They were also commanded to live alone. Which means this poor guy in Mark 1 was an utter pariah. He'd likely lost contact with his family, had no friends outside of the leper colony, and hadn't experienced being touched by another person in years. No back rubs after lugging furniture upstairs, no hugs on his birthday, no gentle hand wiping his tears away when he broke down and cried.

In light of leprosy's extremely transmittable nature, it would've made complete sense if Jesus had chosen to heal him without any physical contact. Instead, our tenderhearted Savior reaches out and touches the man *before* healing his disfigured body. And Mark qualifies that His touch was *compassionate*, which comes from the Greek root word *splangnon*, meaning entrails or vital organs. Therefore, the way Jesus touches this man no one else would dare to reveals that His response to his pain and loneliness came from His "gut."[32]

Jesus doesn't distance Himself from our distress, y'all. No matter how deep or repulsive our wounds, our Savior's gut instinct is to draw near to them, reach out His tender hands, and heal.

- **WHAT SITUATIONS TEND** to make you feel like you're all alone in the dark?

- **READ ISAIAH 49:15-16** and Psalm 27:10. How does your heart respond to these biblical promises? How have you experienced them personally?

- **READ PSALM 68:5-6.** How would you explain these lyrics to someone who's feeling lonely?

Day 39

JESUS WAS NEVER IN A HURRY

"Come to me, all of you who are weary and burdened, and I will give you rest. Take up my yoke and learn from me, because I am lowly and humble in heart, and you will find rest for your souls. For my yoke is easy and my burden is light." MATTHEW 11:28–30

WHEN I WAS AN adolescent, I spent most weekends at my dad's ranch (my parents divorced when I was little), which was in Central Florida in the middle of nowhere. The ranch was a great place to ride horses and motorcycles or chase roosters and fireflies. The only downside to life on the ranch was its isolation and the lack of friends my age. Fortunately, several kind (albeit older and rather rowdy) kids from the youth group at the country church we attended befriended me. And they were more than glad to tutor a straitlaced "city girl" in the art of mild rural rebellion.

One of the most memorable incidents from my brief apprenticeship in crime involved a pickup truck full of green oranges, a passing Volkswagen "VW bug," and peer pressure. It was a hot, summer afternoon and we had all piled into the back of Chris's truck (Chris was a very sweet and unwitting rural Romeo—he was so stinkin' cute but seemingly oblivious that all the girls in the county had a crush on him!) to go get drinks and snacks from Roach's Grocery. (I'm not making this stuff up—that really was the name of the convenience store and the tiny community where it was located was called "Roachville.") The store was about five miles from our ranch, and we chatted and threw oranges at street signs while Chris drove.

Mind you, we weren't planning to do anything destructive . . . until a little red bubble appeared on the horizon of County Road 46A, getting bigger and rounder as we barreled toward it. It looked like a rolling bull's-eye. Someone leaned down and scooped up a shirt-full of oranges to hurl at the bug, and we all followed suit. Everyone's fruity ammo missed the mark and bounced harmlessly off the blacktop—until the very last orange was tossed. The one I threw! Mine hit the road in front of the oncoming car and bounced up for a direct hit in the middle of the windshield.

The other driver slammed on the brakes and whipped around in hot pursuit as we jumped up and down in the back of the truck, screaming as if our lives depended on outrunning him. But an old truck full of teenagers is no match for a Beetle bent on revenge so he caught up with us quickly! Still, we begged Chris to keep driving, "Come on Chris, keep going! Faster, faster!" Although we had probably topped out at thirty miles per hour and the Volkswagen was inches from the rear bumper, we didn't want to stop because the forward motion kept us from facing reality. But after a mile or so, we finally pulled over and I hung my head to confess to the irate driver. Then we turned the truck around and wobbled back home—without so much as a soda—to face my dad.

While I don't make a habit of hurling citrus in traffic anymore, I still tend to race as fast as I can through each day. And my frenetic activity fits right into most Christian circles since we tend to wrap verses around our inability to rest and call it a virtue. We emphasize the "go out and do" passages but ignore the "be still and know" parts. We wear signs of physical exertion like badges of honor, as if all our stress "on God's behalf" is adding up like frequent flyer miles. And the busiest beavers in church are often labeled the best—until their exhaustion begets disillusionment and they limp away, seeking a less demanding pond. Frankly, some of the most stressed out, emotionally spent people I've ever met are Christ-followers.

> "Are you tired? Worn out? Burned out on religion? Come to me. Get away with me and you'll recover your life. *I'll show you how to take a real rest. Walk with me and work with me—watch how I do it. Learn the unforced rhythms of grace.*" (Matt. 11:28–29 MSG, emphasis mine)

During the second to last class of my doctoral candidacy, one of my wonderful Denver Seminary profs and spiritual mentors, Dr. Brad Strait, effectively nailed me to my chair with this simple observation: "Jesus's earthly ministry happened at the pace of approximately 3 mph because He walked everywhere." In all my years of study and pouring over the Bible, I'd never once thought about the pace of our Messiah's praxis. How He never missed a "God moment"—well, because *He is God!*—but besides that massive theological given, Jesus did life with the unforced rhythm of grace. He lived unhurriedly enough to be beautifully interruptible. Lepers were able to ask Him for help when He and the disciples ambled past on their way to town. He sat still long enough for children to climb into His lap and giggle. He looked deep into lonely people's eyes because He wasn't staring at His phone.

Sometimes rest involves a complete cessation of activity, like when we practice a regular Sabbath based on biblical parameters, but sometimes it doesn't. Sometimes it just takes a few minutes to stop and evaluate how fast we're going, then slowing down to match Jesus's pace. I don't know what your goals look like when it comes to slowing down in our lightning-fast world, but my goal is to live the rest of my life—or at least long stretches of it—at 3 mph. Wanna join me?

- **ON A SCALE** of 1 to 10, with 1 being *languid* and 10 being *running around like a chicken with your head cut off*, how would you rate the pace of your life right now?

- **WHAT'S ONE CONCERN,** responsibility, or activity you could set aside— even momentarily—to carve out a bit more breathing room in your life?

- **READ HEBREWS 4:11–13** and 1 Corinthians 10:1–13. What's the common theme of these two passages and what does it imply regarding the relationship between obedience and rest?

Day 40

JESUS IS THE SUPREME HEART SURGEON

He heals the brokenhearted and
bandages their wounds. PSALM 147:3

— , • — —

I'VE EXPERIENCED A FEW minor but ongoing physical consequences since the week I was hospitalized with COVID in 2021, so my doctor recently suggested that I get a full cardiovascular workup to ensure there was no heart damage. The bad news is I was forced to wear paper gowns that had been manufactured based on a supermodel's proportions. The good news is that my ticker is totally fine! But while I was lying in a metal tube with sensors glued to my chest listening to that vital organ somewhere under my sternum thump steadily, I got to thinking about how many times the heart is the highlight of a Bible passage or story.

So I looked it up when I got home and discovered that the word *heart* is liberally scattered throughout Scripture almost one thousand times, which is more often than I say "y'all" even on a verbose day! In the original Old Testament scrolls, the Hebrew word for heart is *léb,* which refers to one's inner self and disposition, and in the original Greek text of the New Testament, the word for heart is *kardia,* from which we get English words like cardiologist.[33] Although the context of the word *heart* in biblical language is usually more spiritual and emotional than physiological—for example, when King David confesses his sin and begs God to give him a clean heart after he gets busted for having an affair with Bathsheba (Ps. 51:10).

Obviously, we won't peruse every verse in which the heart is mentioned in Holy Writ but here's a few I found interesting:

> "So give your servant *a receptive heart* to judge your people and to discern between good and evil. For who is able to judge this great people of yours?" (1 Kings 3:9, emphasis mine)

Which reveals that our hearts can be receptive;

For the High and Exalted One, who lives forever, whose name is holy, says this: "I live in a high and holy place, and with the oppressed and lowly of spirit, to revive the spirit of the lowly and *revive the heart* of the oppressed." (Isa. 57:15, emphasis mine)

Which reveals that our hearts can be revived;

"I will give you a new heart and put a new spirit within you; I will remove *your heart of stone* and give you *a heart of flesh*." (Ezek. 36:26, emphasis mine)

Which reveals that our hearts can be hard or soft;

A joyful heart is good medicine, but a broken spirit dries up the bones. (Prov. 17:22, emphasis mine)

Which reveals that our hearts can be joyful;

He will not fear bad news; *his heart is confident*, trusting in the LORD. (Ps. 112:7, emphasis mine)

Which reveals that our hearts can be confident;

During the month of Nisan in the twentieth year of King Artaxerxes, when wine was set before him, I took the wine and gave it to the king. I had never been sad in his presence, so the king said to me, "Why do you look so sad, when you aren't sick? This is nothing but *sadness of heart*." (Neh. 2:1–2, emphasis mine)

Which reveals that our hearts can be sad;

But some of the scribes were sitting there, *questioning in their hearts*: "Why does he speak like this? He's blaspheming! Who can forgive sins but God alone?" (Mark 2:6–7, emphasis mine)

Which reveals that our hearts can be skeptical; and,

But Mary was *treasuring up all these things in her heart and meditating on them.* (Luke 2:19, emphasis mine)

Which reveals that our hearts can be reflective—and even repositories for truth.

In light of the myriad of emotions that can flow through these four-chambered miracles in our chests and the fact that our Savior is the supreme heart surgeon (and the one whose heart *our* hearts are becoming more like as we grow in our faith), I thought it could be helpful to spend the rest of this devotion doing a sort of spiritual EKG, especially since we don't have to don paper gowns to do so!

1. When I think about how much Jesus loves me, I . . .

2. Being "completely safe" with Jesus would mean I . . .

3. In my relationship with Jesus, I wish I could . . .

4. When I'm moving toward Jesus, I . . .

5. Hearing His voice is sometimes hard for me because . . .

6. Becoming more intimate in my relationship with Jesus would mean I . . .

7. Reflecting on how much time I spend alone with Jesus, I feel . . .

8. I think the main thing that hinders my relationship with Jesus is . . .

9. What I long to consistently experience with Jesus is . . .

10. The last time I felt held by Jesus I . . .

Day 41

JESUS SPEAKS VOLUMES IN OUR SILENCE AND SOLITUDE

Be silent before the LORD and wait expectantly for him . . . PSALM 37:7A

———————

WHILE FILMING A WOMEN'S talk show with CeCe Winans recently, I kept getting distracted by how beautiful and startlingly white her teeth are. So during one of the breaks, I complimented her about it and, to CeCe's humble dismay, one of our other friends on the show announced: "Well, *of course* she has a beautiful smile, Lisa, *she was on a Crest commercial, for goodness' sake!*" Which led to an animated conversation about how super-white teeth make smiles appear happier, which is also the reason I responded to a text ad from my dentist about a sale on professional teeth whitening. (You'll see why I needed a scapegoat in a second.)

Unfortunately, one of his new, inexperienced, and seemingly harried hygienists didn't prep my mouth correctly, which caused the incredibly potent bleaching product to leak onto both the inside and outside of my lower lip. Therefore, instead of coming out of the procedure with a sparkling smile like CeCe's, I came out with a mouth full of blisters and a lip so pronounced that a strong breeze could've pulled me off my feet. Honestly, my bottom lip was so swollen that *I. Could. Not. Talk.* for several hours and Missy had to return a few important calls on my behalf! Which some might call a blessing because I am a grade A-certified *gabber,* y'all.

Since I'm an extroverted windbag by nature, sometimes Jesus's voice in my mind and heart is drowned out by all the words tumbling out of my mouth. Which is why I started practicing the three spiritual disciplines listed below that have really helped me hear Him more often and more clearly. If you're a naturally quiet and contemplative person who doesn't ever have a difficult time discerning the Good Shepherd's voice, please feel free to skip the rest of this devotion and watch a funny animal video on YouTube instead. But for the rest of us, let's move full steam ahead!

1. Silence and Solitude

One of my heroines of the faith, Madame Jeanne Guyon, said this about the two kinds of people who keep silent: "The first is one who has nothing to say, and the other is one who has too much to say. In the case of the deeper encounter with the Lord, the latter is true. Silence is produced from abundant life in God, not from lack."[34] This compelled me to at least try to carve out some quiet each day, even after my lip shrank back to its normal size.

I begin by getting up early, making a cup of coffee, and sitting in a rocking chair on our front porch. Since we live in a rural area, on a hilly five-acre "farmette" without any close neighbors, solitude isn't too hard to come by. Then I spend a chunk of time (sometimes I only have ten minutes, sometimes I have the luxury of an hour) without any noise or activity, and imagine Jesus sitting in the rocking chair next to me. And it's in those quiet moments on the porch with Him that I find the following observation from the book *Cultivating a Listening Heart* to be comfortingly true: "In solitude we have for companionship the One who loves us and who is eager to empower us to do good. As we become used to it, it's not unusual to sit in silence with God as we might with an old friend."[35]

2. Prayer of Examen

I started practicing the prayer of examen (*examen* is simply the Latin root for "examine," and is typically still used in the context of spiritual disciplines because most of them were established by priests and monks centuries ago when religious writings were in Latin) about twenty years ago, and I normally do it in the evening. I begin by quoting Psalm 139:23–24 (NIV): "Search me, God, and know my heart; test me and know my anxious thoughts. See if there is any offensive way in me, and lead me in the way everlasting." After which, I follow the following steps for the General Examen of Conscience:[36]

- Give Jesus thanks for how He's blessed me throughout the day
- Ask Him to reveal my sins
- Examine the posture of my heart during the day, reflecting briefly on my thoughts, words, and actions

- Ask Him to forgive my sins, in light of His unconditional love and mercy
- Ask Him for the grace to change in such a way that I lean more fully into His embrace and live a more Jesus-shaped life

Sometimes Missy joins me in the prayer of examen exercise and, when she does, I simplify the steps down to these three:

- Share the "rose" (the best part) and the "thorn" (the hardest part) of our day
- Thank Jesus for the rose(s)
- Ask Jesus for help with the thorn(s)

3. Walking Prayer

I've found this spiritual discipline to be an awesome way to listen to Jesus *and* work off calories consumed from chips and queso at the same time! At the beginning of walks or hikes that I typically take a few times a week, I practice deep breathing—consciously inhaling God's life and peace through my nose and exhaling anxiety through my mouth several times. (Remember the original Greek word for Holy "Spirit" in the New Testament is *pneuma,* which means breath, so deep breathing doesn't have to be some weird, anti-God thing—it's actually biblically defensible! God used His own breath to fill Adam with the "breath of life" in Genesis 2:7, and in my breathing practices, I remember He is still the One who breathes life into me too!) Then I start walking and repeat whatever verses I've been meditating on (sometimes out loud, sometimes just in my head) for several strides, after which I ask Jesus what He wants to tell me through them, and listen for several minutes while trying to keep my breathing and strides rhythmic. Then I proclaim what I think He's teaching me, convicting me of, encouraging me with, or revealing to me through those passages while keeping a harmonious cadence. And I repeat those steps for the entirety of the walk/hike.

His presence has become so palpable on those prayer walks/hikes that I've been embarrassed more than once when rounding a corner on a trail only to find other hikers staring in consternation because they heard me in animated conversation and assumed I was talking to a companion. So when I come into view without one, they think I've been chattering away to myself and am a few sandwiches short of a picnic!

- **WHAT IS YOUR** rose and your thorn today?

- **READ PSALM 62:5-6.** Take three deep breaths, focusing on breathing in God's peace and exhaling worry or stress. What do you think Jesus is saying to you through these verses?

- **READ JAMES 5:7-8.** Take three deep breaths, focusing on breathing in God's peace and exhaling worry or stress. What do you think Jesus is saying to you through these verses?

Day 42

JESUS DOESN'T PLAY WITH SNAKES

"Woe to you, teachers of the law and Pharisees, you hypocrites! You shut the door of the kingdom of heaven in people's faces. You yourselves do not enter, nor will you let those enter who are trying to." MATTHEW 23:13 NIV

LATE ONE SUNDAY AFTERNOON several summers ago as I was ferrying luggage inside from a weekend trip, I went to the restroom in the middle of unloading. Moments later I was washing my hands and noticed movement out of the corner of my eye in the doorway between my bathroom and bedroom. I glanced over and then screamed because there was a huge snake with about a third of its body reared up in the air, lunging toward me and striking repeatedly. I immediately began backing up and then panicked when I realized I was pretty much trapped in the bathroom because what appeared to be a hostile five- to six-foot rattlesnake was blocking my way out!

I've been in several car accidents, have swum with sharks off the coast of Belize, and stand on a scale in the doctor's office at least once a year, yet I've never felt such sheer terror. I could feel the blood pounding in my ears, and it felt like there was a band tightening around my chest. I cried, "Jesus, help me!" out loud several times, and tried to control my racing mind. But before I could calm down, the snake started slithering toward me and all I could think to do was snatch the plunger from under the sink and try to joust him away. Things went from bad to worse when he sank his fangs into the black rubber and got stuck. I hurled the whole nightmarish heap back toward the doorway, and as Mr. Wiggly laid still, momentarily stunned, I jerked open the linen closet, grabbed a giant beach towel, threw it on top of him, vaulted over the wriggling horror scene like an Olympic hurdler, and raced out of the house.

Fortunately, a chivalrous male friend soon came to my rescue and captured the beast in a Home Depot bucket (but only after being lunged at twice himself, which sort of justified me breathing into a paper bag), then chopped it up in pieces with a shovel in the backyard. He mused that the snake had likely slithered up through the chimney from the crawl space under the house to escape from the extreme summer temperatures. He assured me that while it was over five feet in length, it wasn't poisonous after all (it was a *rat* snake, not a rattlesnake!) and went on to explain that it was probably so aggressive because I'd unwittingly stepped on it when I walked into the restroom, as evidenced by the big footprint indention on his back. In other words, that nasty creature was simply protecting itself from being stomped again or plunged by a big, shrieking human. However, I didn't feel too bad about scaring it and didn't shed a tear during its dissection ceremony.

And while that might sound insensitive, I'm sticking to my guns/plunger because I'm convinced our Savior didn't like slithery things with fangs much either. Which is evidenced by His scathing rebukes of Pharisees who were posing as God's chosen ambassadors but were secretly doing everything in their power to keep seekers from salvation:

> *"Brood of vipers!* How can you speak good things when you are evil?"* (Matt. 12:34a, emphasis mine)

> *"Snakes! Brood of vipers!* How can you escape being condemned to hell?"* (Matt. 23:33, emphasis mine)

Of course, the point here isn't about reptiles—they're merely a metaphor— it's about not messing around with *poisonous people* who try to block our way to Jesus. Furthermore, the notion that Jesus was a nonconfrontational doormat is *not* remotely biblically defensible! Our Savior didn't put up a fight during His betrayal, arrest, bogus trial, and crucifixion (although He could've annihilated the entire Roman army with a flick of His pinky) because Easter is why He came at Christmas in the first place. It was His divine mission to lay down His life and atone for sinners so that through faith in Him we can be reconciled into a right relationship with God (Mark 10:45). But Jesus didn't hesitate from shoving dangerous predators away from His beloved sheep. He didn't play around with two-footed snakes, and we shouldn't either.

- **READ 1 TIMOTHY 6:20-21.** How would you apply Paul's counsel to modern-day entertainment (for example, overtly anti-Christian podcasts, television shows, Internet content, and people you follow on social media)?

- **READ ROMANS 16:17.** How would you communicate this to a kid who's being bullied by classmates in school for being a Christian?

- **READ 1 PETER 3:15–16.** Since this passage (and many, many more throughout the entirety of Scripture) clearly calls Christians to share the living hope of Jesus Christ with the lost and lonely world around us, how can we do so while simultaneously avoiding "snakes"? (Remember, a lost person may very well seek salvation, while a snake tries to block seekers from salvation or lead them astray on purpose. This distinction helps us in our discernment with different types of people!)

Day 43
JESUS IS A SAFE REFUGE TO RUN TO

*<u>God is our refuge</u> and strength, a helper who is always found
in times of trouble.* PSALM 46:1, EMPHASIS MINE

*But I will sing of your strength and will joyfully proclaim your faithful love in the morning. For
you have been a stronghold for me, <u>a refuge in my day of trouble</u>.* PSALM 59:16, EMPHASIS MINE

*Because God wanted to show his unchangeable purpose even more clearly to the heirs
of the promise, he guaranteed it with an oath, so that through two unchangeable things,
in which it is impossible for God to lie, <u>we who have fled for refuge</u> might have strong
encouragement to seize the hope set before us.* HEBREWS 6:17–18, EMPHASIS MINE

YOU KNOW THOSE BUMPER cars at the county fair—the ones that keep
you from getting hurt even when you purposely T-bone one of your friends in
another bumper car after consuming too much sugar from funnel cakes? Well,
an older, much wiser, licensed Christian counselor named Lynn has been my
proverbial bumper for twenty years. She's semi-retired at this point after having
spent decades as a school administrator and then several more in private practice
helping hundreds of people in Middle Tennessee navigate toward Jesus through
the rapture and rupture of real life. In fact, it was my pastor who referred me
to Lynn all those years ago with the ringing endorsement: "God chose Lynn to
single-handedly save my marriage. If it weren't for the grace and wisdom He
poured through her, Darlene and I wouldn't have made it." Fortunately, she still
sees a few clients a week, for which I'm super grateful because I've still got a few
dents in my fender of a heart!

About sixteen years ago Lynn counseled me to make some significant changes
that I didn't. It wasn't that I was trying to be oppositional or anything (goodness
knows I hate to disappoint people, which I've also had to process in therapy!),
but I simply didn't have the emotional maturity or resolve to back up from a
few relationships that were toxic for everyone involved. I was too afraid that
stepping out of the drama I'd been enmeshed in for a long time would be like
pulling the proverbial thread in a sweater and cause my whole world to unravel.

However a few years later, after the relational earthquake she'd forecast in my life occurred and I was shaken to the core, she gently reiterated the same wise, biblical counsel she'd given me long before. What she did *not* do was tell me, "I told you so." Not once. Instead, she provided a safe refuge where I could fall apart and allow the Holy Spirit to put me back together again.

The most common words for *refuge* are the Hebrew verb *ḥāsâ* (which means trust) and the derived noun *maḥseh* (which loosely means protection or fortified tower). Those two terms occur in tandem thirty-four times in the Psalms, and scholars say that their repeated usage indicates that our spiritual ancestors understood it was difficult to trust every outcome of their lives to God.[37] Therefore, they reminded themselves on a regular basis that His presence was the only safe place to be in when they were scared or falling apart!

Speaking of falling apart, the disciple I've always identified with the most is Peter. Which makes sense in view of his verbose tendencies and similar habit of putting his foot in his motormouth on a regular basis! But I can also relate to his more serious issues, which reared their ugly head on the heels of the Last Supper soon after he dramatically declared to Jesus that he'd be faithful to Him forever, even if it meant facing his own death (Matt. 26:35). Because instead of acting like the ride-or-die hero he boasted to be, he threw Jesus under the bus by vehemently and vulgarly betraying Him to try to save his own neck as the harsh reality of the crucifixion began to unfold (Mark 14:66–72).

It would make perfect sense for Pete to have his disciple card revoked and his relationship with the Messiah annulled, wouldn't it? But that's not how the story goes. Instead, only a week or so later, when he's out fishing with the other disciples—surely still overwhelmed with guilt from his betrayal and grief from Jesus's death—Pete recognizes that the person talking to them from the beach is actually the resurrected Messiah. He then leaps out of the boat, swims as fast as he can toward shore, and *runs* toward his Savior (John 21). Remember, this is the first time Pete's seen Jesus since he denied Him. It would've made more since had Pete swam in the opposite direction, hightailed it out of town, and not come back to face Jesus until he'd done some serious penance and could prove he'd dealt with his junk. But he doesn't. Because after spending three years with the King of all kings, he'd witnessed the compassionate character of Christ more times than he could count. Therefore, despite his egregious error(s), Pete knew he'd find mercy at our Savior's feet. And boy, did he! Jesus radically restored that ancient Benedict Arnold—assuring him that He wasn't kicking him off the team, but was naming him team captain—and He didn't even *mention* Peter's epic fail when He did so!

Human nature presumes that the kind of guaranteed safety afforded by an impenetrable fortress would be available only to the honorable who've earned it. To those who fight gallantly instead of fail miserably. To those honest enough to admit their frailties before they're glaringly apparent. To those who follow wise directions immediately, instead of years down the road after they've careened off a cliff. But our Savior's nature is altogether different. Jesus opens the refuge of His arms wide to traitors like us and never, ever says, "I told you so," even though He knows every single stupid, deceitful, cowardly thing we did that got us in trouble in the first place.

- **OUTSIDE OF JESUS,** who is your safest relationship? What makes you feel safe with him/her?

- **READ PSALM 61:4.** How would you put this lyric in your own words?

- **READ MATTHEW 23:37.** Although the context of Matthew 23 is about how the religious leaders in Jerusalem were preoccupied with looking spiritual instead of loving God, what does Jesus's usage of the "hen and chicks" metaphor tell you about His heart?

Day 44

JESUS COMPELS US TO
RECOGNIZE OUR NEEDINESS

*While he was reclining at the table in the house, many tax collectors and sinners
came to eat with Jesus and his disciples. When the Pharisees saw this, they asked
his disciples, "Why does your teacher eat with tax collectors and sinners?"*

*Now when he heard this, he said, "It is not those who are well who need a doctor,
but those who are sick. Go and learn what this means: I desire mercy and not
sacrifice. For I didn't come to call the righteous, but sinners."* MATTHEW 9:10–13

SEVERAL YEARS AGO, I was signing books at a conference and noticed a woman hovering about twenty feet away. Every time I looked up, she glanced nervously in my direction, so as soon as I could, I walked over and introduced myself. She was wearing a waitress uniform that had seen better days, and explained how she'd come to the event straight from her morning shift at a pancake house. Then she shyly confessed that she identified with the stories I'd shared about my friends in addiction recovery. She went on to explain that she'd been addicted to meth for six years and had gotten clean by the grace of God.

After explaining that what I'd said about Jesus loving broken people and how our pasts don't determine our destiny really blessed her, she pressed a crumpled twenty-dollar bill in my hand and said, "I wish I had more to give you, but please take this and use it for gas so you can go more places and tell more people like me that Jesus loves them." At that point all I knew about her was what she'd shared in the span of three or four minutes, so I can't be sure about this, but I assumed she needed that cash more than I did.

I mean, good night, I've got medical insurance, get manicures every couple of weeks, and had driven there in a car that was only a few years old. I felt guilty and awkward taking money from a woman who'd obviously been through heck and back and appeared to need it more than I did. So I replied gently, "Thank you so much, ma'am, but your encouragement is more than enough of a gift," and tried to press the bill back into her closed fist. And instantly regretted my response when a look of disappointment washed across her face. When she leaned closer and whispered, "Please, I really want to help," I accepted the bill with the gravitas a sacrificial gift like hers deserved and hugged her for a long time. My throat was tight with tears when we said goodbye, but I managed to thank her again and told her that her generosity had helped me more than she could possibly know. The lesson God engraved on my heart that day was, while I didn't necessarily need the gas money, I desperately needed a friend to pull me out of the rut of self-sufficiency I'd once again gotten stuck in.

I'm so much more comfortable helping those in need than admitting I need help. Heck, even though I'm pushing sixty, I still usually run my own chainsaw when storms damage trees on our property rather than call a tree service. And while I've held my own with saplings and smaller trees, I have some gnarly scars to prove that trying to cut down a huge cedar was a bonehead move on my part! I've had to learn the hard way that pretending I don't need help when I'm in way over my head isn't just dumb, it's dangerous. Which is certainly the case of the Pharisees who turned up their noses at the people who were enjoying a meal with Jesus: "When the Pharisees saw this, they asked his disciples, 'Why does your teacher eat with tax collectors and sinners?'" (Matt. 9:11).

You can almost hear the condescension in their question, can't you? It's important to note here that Pharisees considered anyone who didn't interpret and codify Torah exactly the same way they did as a "sinner." Plus, they had super-strict laws regarding cleanliness and ritual washing. Which means these folks chowing down with our Savior weren't necessarily notorious delinquents with threadbare morals; they may have simply forgotten to wash their hands before they ate.[38] When Jesus said, "It is not those who are well who need a doctor, but those who are sick" (v. 12), He wasn't celebrating the low cholesterol level of Pharisees, He was using irony to illuminate their inability to admit they needed spiritual healing. And when He said, "I didn't come to call the righteous, but sinners" (v. 13b), He wasn't rebuffing the righteous, He was trying to help that haughty "God squad" recognize they needed as much divine aid as the tax collectors and non-hand-washers they judged as inferior. In short, Jesus was trying to make it clear that God's salvific help comes to those who are open to *receiving* it.

Neediness is a spiritual necessity, y'all. Regardless of how well we toe the line—whether we're like those ancient religious leaders who dotted every spiritual "i" and crossed every spiritual "t" or we're more on the motley crew side of things—ultimately, we can't save ourselves. In fact, whatever claim we make to "righteousness" is equivalent to a bunch of filthy rags (Isa. 64:6 NIV)! No matter who we are or what rung of the societal ladder we were brought up on, our merciful Messiah compels us to acknowledge how sin has made our souls sick because He longs to make us well.

- **DO YOU TEND** to be more comfortable giving help or receiving help? Why do you think that is?

- **READ JOHN 5:1-9.** How would you answer the question Jesus asked the paralytic?

- **READ 2 CHRONICLES 7:14.** What does this verse reveal about the relationship between humility and healing?

JESUS VALUES PEOPLE OVER PROTOCOL

Moving on from there, he entered their synagogue. There he saw a man who had a shriveled hand, and in order to accuse him they asked him, "Is it lawful to heal on the Sabbath?"

He replied to them, "Who among you, if he had a sheep that fell into a pit on the Sabbath, wouldn't take hold of it and lift it out? A person is worth far more than a sheep; so it is lawful to do what is good on the Sabbath."

Then he told the man, "Stretch out your hand." So he stretched it out, and it was restored, as good as the other. But the Pharisees went out and plotted against him, how they might kill him. MATTHEW 12:9–14

———————

DURING DECEMBER 2022 MILLIONS of people in America experienced some of the coldest few days on record, but the hearty citizens of Buffalo, New York, were hit especially hard. They endured what their governor (a Buffalo native) described as the longest sustained blizzard to ever hit the city. Conditions there were so harsh that emergency workers were unable to get to many people who'd lost power in their homes or motorists who were stranded on roads, resulting in dozens of tragic deaths. But there were some bright moments during that frigid season in upstate New York, too, including a heartwarming story about a "criminal" who became a hero.

> *To Whomever It May Concern:*
>
> *I'm terribly sorry for breaking the school window and for breaking in the kitchen. Got stuck at 8 p.m. on Friday and slept in my truck with two strangers. Just trying not to die. There were 7 elderly people also stuck and out of fuel. I had to do it to save everyone and get them shelter and food and a bathroom. Merry Christmas.*
>
> *Jay*

This note with no last name that was left in a school outside Buffalo on Christmas Day 2022 prompted an enthusiastic search by the Cheektowaga Police Department to find "Jay." And because of video surveillance footage from the school he broke into, it didn't take long! His name is Jay Withey Jr. He's a twenty-seven-year-old appliance mechanic and is credited with saving the lives of at least twenty people during that ferocious winter storm. After taking a stranded child and an elderly woman into his truck overnight on December 23, he got up the next morning and made his way to Pine Hill Primary Center school, where he broke a classroom window, climbed inside, opened a door, and then went back outside into the blinding snow, howling wind, and subzero temperatures for his two passengers and trudged through hip-deep drifts from car to car to help usher other stranded motorists to safety inside the heated school, where they spent the next twenty-four hours waiting out the storm together.

Jay and his new friends ate small servings of frozen pizza, cereal, and fruit from the school cafeteria and took some medicine from the nurse's office, but were scrupulous about only using what they needed to survive. After the worst of the weather broke on Christmas Day, they cleaned up after themselves, washed the dishes and pans they'd used (school officials said it was hard to tell anyone had even been there, save for the broken window they had carefully boarded up before leaving), helped dig each other's cars out, and traveled on to their respective destinations.

The Cheektowaga Central School District and the police have chosen not to press charges. And I'd bet my bottom dollar there was no angel holding a clipboard in Glory chalking up Jay's behavior as sin either!

Because throughout the Gospels Jesus consistently put people over protocol and relationships over regulations. Which is evidenced by the healing encounter Jesus had smack-dab in the middle of a synagogue on the Sabbath. The very place the Pharisees (from the original Greek word *pharisaios,* which means, "separate ones"[39]) practiced Sabbath and interpreted the Hebrew Scriptures into a codified list of rigid behavioral guidelines. Which means that nasty habit of taking God's Word out of context and twisting it into a club with which to beat people up has been around long before we were!

Anyway, those persnickety Pharisees single out this poor man with the hurt hand and ask: *What do you think about healing this guy right here, right now, Yeshua?* And their query exposes their desire to trap Jesus in a theological paradox because there's a well-established principle in Jewish tradition that physical healing—which was regarded as "work"—was forbidden on the Sabbath except in life-threatening situations.[40] Therefore, since this man wasn't in danger of dying, the Pharisees callously picked him out as bait.

In my somewhat sanctified imagination, Jesus regards those zealous legalists with a slow, sad smile. Then He patiently explains that since there are exceptions in Torah for pulling a stranded animal out of a ditch on the Sabbath, surely, it's all right with our Father in heaven when we extend compassion to someone who's in obvious distress *in church*. And as those ancient deacons stand there all sweaty and flummoxed, unsure of how to retort, He heals the disfigured man.

Jesus was preoccupied with caring for people, not checking off boxes on some kind of "religious procedures" form—ones that weren't even true to the Scriptures, but were rather man-made traditions! And while I'm not advocating that we add breaking and entering to our small group agendas unless *absolutely* necessary, I do think we must be willing to hurl our inner rule books if they get in the way of helping the wounded world around us!

- **WHAT FRIEND, FAMILY** member, or spiritual leader comes to mind when you think about someone who puts people over protocol? What about them reveals that?

- **READ JOHN 5:39.** What's the gist of Jesus's accusation here? What kind of behavior exemplifies knowing the Bible but totally missing the point about loving God and people?

- **READ 1 JOHN 4:20.** How would you paraphrase this to someone who's interested in/investigating the claims of Christianity?

Day 46

JESUS IS EXCLUSIVELY BOTH LORD *AND* CHRIST

*"This Jesus God raised up, and of that we all are witnesses. Being therefore
exalted at the right hand of God, and having received from the Father the promise
of the Holy Spirit, he has poured out this that you yourselves are seeing and
hearing. For David did not ascend into the heavens, but he himself says,*

*"'The Lord said to my Lord,
"Sit at my right hand,
until I make your enemies your footstool."'*

*Let all the house of Israel therefore know for certain that <u>God has made him both
Lord and Christ, this Jesus</u> whom you crucified."* ACTS 2:32–36 ESV, EMPHASIS MINE

———

WHEN I WAS IN my late thirties, I decided that if I didn't have a husband by
the significant milestone of forty, I was going to get a Harley Davidson. I've
been hooked on motorcycles for most of my life, beginning with a Honda 70
minibike my dad got me for Christmas when I was seven or eight, much to my
mom's chagrin. But I'd never housed a "Hog" in the garage (biker slang term for
a Harley Davidson), which in some rider-enthusiast circles is the equivalent of
saying you like to swim but have never been in water!

Long story short, no one I fancied asked for my hand in marriage in my
pre-forty season, so I ultimately bought a super cool, chromed-out, anniversary
edition Harley. And one of the first lessons I learned after becoming an official
Hog owner is that a lot of folks who ride them are quite obsessive about the
uniqueness of brand and don't take kindly to non-Harley riders wearing the
emblem on hats or T-shirts. The attitude of most Harley dudes and dudettes I
know is: "Ours is the only kind of bike worth having and if you don't ride one,
don't fly our flag!"

Which is basically the point Peter was making about Jesus, too, when he
bellowed:

> "Let all the house of Israel therefore know for certain that *God has
> made him both Lord and Christ, this Jesus* whom you crucified."
> (Acts 2:36 ESV, emphasis mine)

This speech from Peter (the first of two, actually) is so packed full of amazing stuff, it's like drinking from a fire hose of grace! In fact, before this former failure of a disciple even opened his mouth, Luke describes him as "standing" up (Acts 2:14 ESV), a term in the original Greek which indicates not only the physical posture of rising, but a "rising up" in character.[41] In other words, the very same man who threw Jesus under the bus after His bogus arrest in the garden of Gethsemane now bravely faces a massive crowd and preaches the first public, post-resurrection message!

Because, remember, that a week or so after the Prince of Peace was nailed to a tree on a hill outside of Jerusalem, the resurrected Christ appeared to Peter and forgave him for his betrayal (John 21). Furthermore, Jesus—who *knew* Peter would fumble the ball on the first yard line—still commissioned him to be the rock He was going to build the early church on (Matt. 16:18). And Pete must've sensed the Lord's mercy and commissioning were sincere despite his mistakes, because out of the eleven apostles who were present at Pentecost, he's the only one who chose to accept the challenge of addressing the gathering and then he preached a very bold, politically incorrect sermon about the supremacy and exclusivity of Jesus! In fact, Peter is the first human in history to assert that Jesus was both "Lord" and "Christ." Prior to Acts 2, *Lord* was a title exclusively ascribed by Jews to Yahweh, the God of Israel, and *Christ* was a title exclusively used by Jews to describe the coming Messiah or "Anointed One." And the Holy Spirit infused Peter's radical claim with so much power and authority that thousands of people responded with repentance and launched themselves into the unconditionally loving arms of Jesus:

> Peter's words pierced their hearts, and they said to him and to the other apostles, "Brothers, what should we do?"
>
> Peter replied, "Each of you must repent of your sins and turn to God, and be baptized in the name of Jesus Christ for the forgiveness of your sins. Then you will receive the gift of the Holy Spirit. This promise is to you, to your children, and to those far away—all who have been called by the Lord our God." Then Peter continued preaching for a long time, strongly urging all his listeners, "Save yourselves from this crooked generation!"
>
> Those who believed what Peter said were baptized and added to the church that day—about 3,000 in all. (Acts 2:37–41 NLT)

Contrary to culture's claims that there are many roads that lead to God, Scripture makes it abundantly clear that there's only One and His name is Jesus. It's only through the narrow gate of a real relationship with Him that we can be reconciled with a holy God. Lord is not Jesus's formal name, nor is Christ His last name. They are His royal titles and convey His supremacy. The gift of eternal salvation is exclusively His to offer.

- **WHAT OTHER "WAYS"** have you heard/been taught that you can find a path to God and spiritual fulfillment?

- **READ JOHN 14:6.** How would you respectfully paraphrase this to an unbeliever?

- **HOW CAN WE** better reconcile our belief in the exclusivity of salvation through Jesus Christ alone with the grace and respect He clearly calls us to extend toward those who don't yet know Him?

Day 47
JESUS WEPT

As soon as Mary came to where Jesus was and saw him, she fell at his feet and told him, "Lord, if you had been here, my brother wouldn't have died!"

When Jesus saw her crying, and the Jews who had come with her crying, he was deeply moved in his spirit and troubled. "Where have you put him?" he asked.

"Lord," they told him, "come and see." <u>Jesus wept.</u>
JOHN 11:32–35, EMPHASIS MINE

I CAN'T REMEMBER LONG stretches of that week I spent in the hospital battling severe pneumonia and lung complications brought on by COVID. I lost entire days to a medicated fog and the white noise of beeping machines. But I can remember almost every detail of the day my pneumatologist finally pronounced me well enough to go home. I remember the wide grins on the faces of the wonderful nursing team who'd selflessly taken care of me when I didn't have enough strength to even say, "Thank you." Of course, part of their happiness may've been due to the huge cake I'd had delivered to them that morning! I also remember how one of the aides (who was given the task of schlepping all the thoughtful "Get Well" paraphernalia out of my room) got frustrated because some of the balloons kept sticking out of the elevator doors when he was trying to close them. But what I remember most is my dear friend Shane, who was standing in a grassy median across from the hospital exit doors (the nearest security would let visitors do this during that season when no one knew exactly what proximity protocols to implement for COVID).

Shane had driven to the hospital immediately after hearing I was being released and had been waiting there in the pouring rain since. The moment she saw me being wheeled outside toward my nephew's waiting car, she began jumping up and down, waving her arms, and cheering with all the gusto one usually reserves for Superbowl champions or Grammy winners. I asked John Michael (my nephew) to drive up next to her when he gingerly pulled away from the hospital so I could see her up close and mouth "Thank you" through the window. And when he did, I realized that the rivulets running down sweet Shane's face weren't from the rain, they were tears.

Crying used to make me uncomfortable. There was so much anger and chaos and sadness in my early childhood before my parents divorced that I subconsciously began using my blanket as a mini cape and tried to be Little Miss Sunshine. The way I figured it, my poor mom and dad already had their hands full of so much hard stuff, they needed a daughter who was a self-sufficient smiler, not some needy crybaby. I was well into adulthood before I finally understood that my childish conviction that "sad = bad" was way off base. Because sincere tears are God's gift to express emotion where words fail. They can carry big, bulky balloon bouquets of sheer joy or help wash the debris of spent sorrow from our weary souls.

When I was a kid, I missed the promise and potency of: *Jesus wept.* Like most of my other buddies in Sunday school, I snickered when a peer quoted it as their "memory verse" because we all knew it was the shortest verse in the Bible and, therefore, a way to cheat in church. But now that the portion of life I have left is significantly less than the portion I've already lived, I find the truth packed in those two words to be profoundly encouraging.

Charles Haddon Spurgeon explained it much better than I can in one of his centuries-old sermons:

> *I have often felt vexed with the man, whoever he was, who chopped up the New Testament into verses. He seems to have let the hatchet drop indiscriminately here and there; but I forgive him a great deal of blundering for his wisdom in letting these two words make a verse by themselves: "Jesus wept." This is a diamond of the first water, and it cannot have another gem set with it, for it is unique. Shortest of verses in words, but where is there a longer one in sense? Add a word to the verse, and it would be out of place. No, let it stand in solitary sublimity and simplicity. You may even put a note of exclamation after it, and let it stand in capitals.*[42]

When I found out that Dr. Spurgeon, who's one of my all-time favorite heroes of the faith, battled with severe depression, my respect for him only grew. My heart softened when I read that despite how 25,000 people bought copies of his sermons every week during the height of his ministry and he got to preach to ten million people before his death in 1892, he still had moments when tears were his only language. As evidenced by how he described his experience after an especially dark season: *there are dungeons beneath the castles of despair.*[43]

Spurgeon's comfort with crying is the main reason I trust his takeaways from John's account of our Savior doing so:

> First, I would remind you that "Jesus wept," because *he was truly man*: secondly, "Jesus wept," for *he was not ashamed of his human weakness*, but allowed himself to reveal the fact that he was, in this point also, made like unto his brethren. Thirdly, "Jesus wept," and therein *he is our instructor*. Fourthly, *he is our comforter*; and lastly, *he is our example*.[44]

We are not loved by a stoic God, y'all. We are celebrated over and empathized with and grieved about and comforted by a compassionate Redeemer. Jesus is deeply moved by our stories and more tender toward us than you and I can possibly imagine or hope for.

- **READ JOHN 3:16** (NIV) out loud. Read it again, emphasizing the word *so*. How does emphasizing that word change the way your heart "hears" this promise?

- **READ ISAIAH 53.** Can you picture *this Jesus* sitting beside you with tears rolling down His face during your deepest season of grief?

- **READ HEBREWS 12:1-2.** Can you picture *this Jesus* teary with joy when you turn back toward Him after a season of wandering?

Day 48

JESUS IS OUR JUBILEE

So all the generations from Abraham to David were <u>fourteen generations</u>; and from David until the exile to Babylon, <u>fourteen generations</u>; and from the exile to Babylon until the Messiah, <u>fourteen generations</u>. MATTHEW 1:17, EMPHASIS MINE

ONE CHRISTMAS A VERY long time ago, when I was in my early twenties and working in youth ministry in Nashville, I barely had enough money for gas to drive home to Central Florida to spend the holidays with my family. So I didn't have much to spend for gifts. It was easy to figure out something inexpensive and creative for Mom because we've always been close, and I knew what would make her feel celebrated and appreciated. But Dad's gift took a little more time. I finally decided that I'd sneak into his house while he was at work and clean it from top to bottom since he was a bachelor by then and not the tidiest of housekeepers. Then, after everything was spick-and-span, I put a small Norfolk Island pine tree in the corner of his living room and decorated it with a strand of lights and twelve notes—all of which I'd written on parchment paper with a calligraphy pen and then rolled up and tied with a red ribbon, each describing a special memory we'd shared and/or something I loved about him.

It was kind of a risky gift because my dad was a gruff man who tended to get uncomfortable around emotion. Well, except in church; Dad *loved* the Pentecostal congregation he went to the last half of his life and most of the folks there were quite wiggly and emotive! But the bottom line is: it would've been a safer bet to just buy him slippers and a wallet like I'd done the year before. I don't remember exactly how he responded when he got home that Christmas Eve and found his house cleaned and the little "Charlie Brown" tree, but thirty years later I found myself cleaning his house from top to bottom again after his funeral. And that's when I knew how he really felt about my modest gift, because when I was wiping at least a decade's worth of dust off his dresser, I found each scroll that he'd carefully saved all those years. They were all yellowed with age but still neatly tied with a faded, red satin ribbon. Sometimes it's the smallest gifts that mean the most, isn't it?

There's one small verse in Matthew's account of the genealogy of Jesus that surely meant a great deal to his original first-century audience, and it still holds huge meaning for us today. We just need to wipe off a couple of millennia's layers worth of dust to find it! When Matthew frames the time leading up to our Savior's birth in spans of fourteen generations, it's all too easy to ignore it as numerological drivel. Given the fact that he was a tax collector before he became a disciple, perhaps he'd never lost the boring habit of using math as a metaphor, right? I mean it's no wonder why Luke's lovely birth narrative with the whole "away in a manger" scene is so much more popular at Christmastime.

"Any text without a context is a pretext for a proof text" (a well-known truism by Dr. D. A. Carson) is the rebar in my theological scaffolding because, if we want to really understand what God was communicating then and how to apply those redemptive truths now, it's imperative for modern-day Christ-followers to know what was going on when the Bible was originally written/spoken. And boy howdy, does that apply to Matthew 1:17!

In order to unwrap this divine present, we've got to remember that numbers were hugely important in Hebraic culture, especially the number seven in light of the Genesis narrative. There are seven holy Jewish festivals; the Sabbath is the seventh day; a *Shemittah* (the Hebrew word for "sabbatical") was to be observed in the seventh year; and their jubilee (which was a celebratory year when certain liberties and freedoms were proclaimed and practiced throughout Israel for both people and even the land) was sometimes referred to as the "Sabbath's Sabbath" because it took place on the last year of seven sabbatical cycles, or the forty-ninth year, according to Leviticus:

> "In addition, *you must count off seven Sabbath years, seven sets of seven years, adding up to forty-nine years in all.* Then on the Day of Atonement in the fiftieth year, blow the ram's horn loud and long throughout the land. Set this year apart as holy, a time to proclaim freedom throughout the land for all who live there. *It will be a jubilee year for you,* when each of you may return to the land that belonged to your ancestors and return to your own clan." (Lev. 25:8–10 NLT, emphasis mine)

Therefore, when Matthew told his version of the Christmas story and said *fourteen, fourteen, fourteen* (and by the way, he was intentional in the way he broke their history down into three equivalent groupings), followed by the Messiah, he was highlighting Jesus as the *seventh seven*. What those precious Jewish people—who'd been bound both by literal captivity, as well as the weight of how their crooked spiritual leaders interpreted Mosaic Law—would've heard and understood is: *Jesus is the Jubilee!* Jesus is the One who brings freedom! Pretty amazing gift, huh?

- **HOW IS JESUS** your Jubilee? What has Jesus set you free from?

- **WHAT—OR WHO—STILL MAKES** you feel trapped?

- **READ GALATIANS 5:1.** Now read it again slowly and out loud if possible (obviously you can omit that part if you're on a crowded plane, train, or automobile!). How does this verse resonate with the reality of where your heart is this season?

JESUS PROPELS US TOWARD
OUR MINISTRY DESTINY

I commend to you our sister Phoebe, who is a servant of the church in Cenchreae. So you should welcome her in the Lord in a manner worthy of the saints and assist her in whatever matter she may require your help. For indeed she has been a benefactor of many—and of me also.

Give my greetings to Prisca and Aquila, my coworkers in Christ Jesus, who risked their own necks for my life. Not only do I thank them, but so do all the Gentile churches. Greet also the church that meets in their home. Greet my dear friend Epaenetus, who is the first convert to Christ from Asia. Greet Mary, who has worked very hard for you. Greet Andronicus and Junia, my fellow Jews and fellow prisoners. They are noteworthy in the eyes of the apostles, and they were also in Christ before me. ROMANS 16:1–7, EMPHASIS MINE

I HAD TO WEAR full leg braces for two years when I was a little girl. They buckled around my waist with a thick leather strap from which protruded heavy steel bars that extended down either side of my bowed legs all the way to my ankles and then looped under my feet inside heavy orthopedic shoes. Remember in the Tom Hanks movie *Forrest Gump*, when the bullies are chasing little Forrest and Jenny yells, "Run, Forrest, Run"? And remember how Forrest's braces fell off when he started running? Well, Forrest and I had identical braces. Only mine didn't miraculously fall off. . . . I had to wear them throughout kindergarten and most of the first grade.

I hated the way those braces made me look as damaged on the outside as I felt on the inside. And I hated missing recess. Almost every day I watched Charlene Williams boot home runs in kickball while I sat stiffly on the sidelines. But then one spring afternoon, the doctor took another set of X-rays and said my bones were finally growing straight and that I didn't have to wear braces anymore.

The next day I lined up with the rest of the kids when they chose teams for kickball. I was fidgety and excited about getting to play again . . . and just a little disappointed when I got picked last. Of course, that made sense. I hadn't been able to run or jump for so long that the other kids naturally assumed I'd be a cruddy kickball player. I can still vividly remember what happened when it was my turn to kick. The outfielders moved in close, thinking I'd be an easy out. The pitcher rolled this red rubber ball toward where I was standing behind home plate and it seemed to get bigger and bigger as it wobbled toward me—and then "boom!"—I kicked that sucker over everybody's head and raced around the bases for a homerun so fast I almost mowed down the kid in front of me. If he hadn't sped up, I'm pretty sure I would've soared right over his head because I felt like I could fly that day!

In today's passage, we see the proverbial braces come flying off of five unlikely ministry home-runners—three of whom are women! A big honkin' surprise given how marginalized women were in Paul's cultural moment. First there's Phoebe, whom Paul calls a "servant"—or *diakonos* in the original Greek, which means, many scholars say, that she was a deacon.

Then there's Priscilla (Prisca), the wife of Aquila, whom Paul refers to as a fellow worker, or *synergos* in the original Greek. Which was a special term Paul only used to describe his close associates in church ministry. In fact, in the book of Acts, Paul lauds Priscilla and Aquila as being able to "[explain] . . . the way of God more adequately" to a fiery, John-the-Baptist like leader in the early church named Apollos (Acts 18:26 NIV), which meant she at least co-mentored other spiritual leaders with her husband. And what's even more interesting is that in four of the six times Priscilla is mentioned in the New Testament, she is listed *before* Aquila! Which is so unusual in New Testament literature that some scholars assert that she was the more prominent one of that dynamic duo!

But I think the most interesting member on God's team of star devil-booty-kicking athletes in Romans 16 is Junia, whom Paul refers to as *"note-worthy in the eyes of the apostles"* (v. 7, emphasis mine) along with Andronicus. In other words, a leader among leaders. However, since it was assumed for centuries that women weren't "supposed" to be leaders, somewhere along the line of biblical translation a gentleman (I'm using considerable restraint here!) who was copying the letter to the Romans changed the original spelling of "Junia"—which was a woman's name in Greco-Roman culture—to "Junias"—which was a man's name in Greco-Roman culture. As a result, for many years it was assumed that Andronicus's buddy and Paul's ministry partner in Romans 16:7 was a dude. However, relatively recent and exhaustive study has pretty much proven that this outstanding leader that the apostles took note of was indeed named Junia and was indeed a woman![45]

Now please know, I don't want to burn my bra and, believe me, you don't want me to either! I'm not trying to shake down any institutions or stir up any more drama when it comes to gender. What I am trying to point out is that if you're firmly rooted in Christ, He'll propel you into your ministry destiny. If God has blessed you with leadership gifts which you've willingly put under the authority of the Holy Spirit, He'll launch you into situations where you can *lead* for His glory. If God has blessed you with serving gifts which you've willingly submitted to the authority of the Holy Spirit, He'll scoot you into settings where you can *serve* for His glory. If God has blessed you with teaching gifts which you've willingly submitted to the authority of the Holy Spirit, He'll lead you toward students you can *teach* for His glory. If God has blessed you with musical gifts which you've willingly submitted to the authority of the Holy Spirit, He'll usher you into environments where you can *sing or play* for His glory. You don't have to sit on the sidelines anymore, the King of all kings had picked you to be on His team, baby!

- **AUTHOR AND THEOLOGIAN** Frederick Buechner once said, "The place God calls you to is the place where your deep gladness and the world's deep hunger meet."[46] Where do you find deep gladness?

- **READ MATTHEW 9:35-38.** What specific gifts do you have that could help bring in a spiritual "harvest"?

- **THE GREEK WORD** for *apostle* is derived from the verb "to send."[47] What do you feel like God is sending you toward during this season of your life?

Day 50

JESUS IS A PROVEN HISTORICAL FIGURE

When Jesus came to the region of Caesarea Philippi, he asked his disciples, "Who do people say that the Son of Man is?" They replied, "Some say John the Baptist; others, Elijah; still others, Jeremiah or one of the prophets." "But you," he asked them, "who do you say that I am?" Simon Peter answered, "<u>You are the Messiah, the Son of the living God</u>." Jesus responded, "Blessed are you, Simon son of Jonah, because flesh and blood did not reveal this to you, but my Father in heaven." MATTHEW 16:13–17, EMPHASIS MINE

WHEN I LIVED IN Colorado in my thirties, I was an avid backpacker. I loved hiking through the mountains and watching a stand of Aspen trees sway in unison in the wind like a choreographed group of dancers. I enjoyed climbing high above the tree line in midsummer and discovering patches of snow that hadn't yet melted, like secret, shimmering diamonds. I savored the sound of high-country creeks tumbling over rocks as they carried melted snow down to the valley below. I was amazed by the gorgeous colors of green and pink refracting on silvery trout scales as they darted about in the crystal clear, freezing cold water. I marveled while I watched the sun set behind one of those beautiful Rocky Mountains I'd been exploring, momentarily leaving a rose gold kiss of last light as it descended. But that's when my ardent love for the great outdoors comes screeching to a halt because I don't even *like* sleeping in a tent in the middle of the wilderness!

Instead, I typically get nervous in the pitch-black of late nights in nature. When an owl's hoots reverberate through the thin mountain air (and the equally thin nylon of a tent), it tends to sound less like an idyllic woodland creature and more like a wild tetradactyl swooping down on its prey. One night, many years ago, my oh-so-patient best friend Judy and I were camped up high in the saddle of Buckskin Pass in the Maroon Bells–Snowmass Wilderness area near Aspen, when I became convinced there was a man-eating monster just outside our tent. Of course, Judy was fast asleep at that point (because she doesn't have the same unfounded-nocturnal-camping-terror disease that I do), so I nudged her sleeping bag and whispered, "Jude, wake up, there's someone out there!" It took several more pokes before she finally rolled over and loudly mumbled grumpily that no one was out there. I emphatically gestured for her to keep her voice down because I didn't want the half-man-half-bear brute who was surely tromping around our campsite just waiting to maul us to *hear us*. At which point, Judy flipped on her headlamp, unzipped the tent opening, scrambled outside, and said with exasperation, "Lisa, there's *nothing* out here!" Which is when we noticed the retreating backside of a marmot (which are basically chunky but harmless ground squirrels!), whose scrounging for food scraps I'd clearly mistaken for a monster with murderous intent.

Far too many folks have been distracted by the scurrying sounds of seemingly fearsome brutes who are intent on disproving the existence of Jesus rather than recognizing the logical and irrefutable truth that He was a historical figure. All it takes is a quick Google search to realize that millions of precious image-bearers are essentially trembling in their tents with the unfounded belief that there's no such thing as a God who loves them so much that He'd leave His throne in Glory, commune with humanity, and ultimately condescend to death on a cross to save them. However, the anti-Jesus scoffers and skeptics—whose volume seems to be steadily increasing in our modern age—aren't telling the whole story when they superciliously cite "facts" in their attempt to prove that an incarnate Messiah never existed.

These night dwellers (whose bark is way worse than their bite, mind you) don't want the world to know about the overwhelming evidence pointing to the legitimacy of Jesus Christ that has been documented not only by the Bible (which we forget is a verifiable historical document on top of being the living Word of God) and Christian historians and archeologists, but also by numerous *non-Christian* sources! Including but not limited to the following list compiled by my theological superhero, seminary professor, and esteemed scholar, Dr. Craig Blomberg:

> A dozen or more references to Jesus appear in non-Christian Jewish, Greek, and Roman sources in the earliest centuries of the Common Era (i.e., from the birth of Jesus onward, as Christianity and Judaism began to overlap chronologically). These references appear in such diverse sources as Josephus (a first-century Jewish historian), several different portions of the Talmud (an encyclopedic collection of rabbinic traditions, finally codified in the fourth through sixth centuries), the Greek writers Lucian of Samosata

and Mara bar Serapion, and Roman historians Thallus, Tacitus, Pliny, and Suetonius.[48]

Dr. Blomberg goes on to qualify this list by explaining that until recent history, ancient historians focused almost exclusively on the exploits of kings and queens, military conquests and defeats, or the elite of any given society. Therefore, the reams of material about this poor Rabbi from a dinky Middle Eastern village (compiled by mostly non-Jewish unbelievers, which means they had *zero motivation* to record the details of His life or perpetuate His message) is impressive.

Of course, there are piles upon piles of additional historical evidence supporting the reality of our Redeemer, as well as the current testimonies of approximately 2.5 *billion* believers! *Christianity is not* an opiate for the weak-minded masses, a figment of our emotive imaginations, or an existential construct for needy people with unfulfilled hopes and dreams, y'all! The great news of the Gospel, and the Savior that stands at the center of it, is truer than true. So may I encourage those of you who've secretly wondered if Jesus really is who you've heard He is—or isn't—to pull back your proverbial tent flap, look past those silly posing erudite thinkers, and responsibly consider the concrete proof of the Christ?

- **REREAD MATTHEW 16:13–17.** How would you answer Jesus's question?

- **HAVE YOU EVER** read a book by a respected academic (like Dr. Craig Blomberg or Dr. Tim Keller or Dr. Craig Keener, for example) about the historical reliability of Jesus? If not, will you consider doing so this season?

- **WHAT ARE THE** loudest questions still lingering in your mind about who Jesus is?

Day 51

JESUS PUT THE PERSONAL IN PRAYER

"Therefore, you should pray like this:

<u>Our Father</u> *in heaven,*
your name be honored as holy.
Your kingdom come.
Your will be done
on earth as it is in heaven.
Give us today our daily bread.
And forgive us our debts,
as we also have forgiven our debtors.
And do not bring us into temptation,
but deliver us from the evil one."
MATTHEW 6:9–15, EMPHASIS MINE

I'M SURE IT COMES as no surprise that I love how my daughter, Missy, prays since I've made it clear that I'm pathologically biased when it comes to her! But if you'll indulge my swollen mama-heart once more, the reason I love eavesdropping on her conversations with God isn't because of how she "performs," it's her refreshingly genuine posture.

Missy prays without pretense. If she's telling Him how my lack of patience has bruised her heart, she doesn't camouflage her feelings with fancy words, but instead shares the unvarnished truth about how she needs His comfort and would like for Him to please help me with my shortcomings. Likewise, if she's confessing one of her own mistakes—such as when she recently spent most of math class doodling her current crush's name on her hand in black marker instead of completing her worksheet—she's forthright about her offense and doesn't feign innocence with poetic sentimentality. And ever since she began learning English after I brought her home from Haiti, she's been concluding her prayers with, "In Jesus's *names.*" I won't correct her either because, quite frankly, I think it's good theology—He does have a lot of names! The bottom line is my sweet sixth-grader communicates with Jesus in the natural language of someone who's in a real relationship with Him.

When Jesus taught the disciples how to pray, He eschewed rigid, distant formality for a much more natural approach as well. As a matter of fact, before we even get to the words our Savior spoke, it's hugely significant to note that the language He addressed Father God in was Aramaic—the language He'd grown up speaking in Nazareth. Other rabbis from ancient times right up until that point would verbalize petitions and praise to Yahweh solely in Hebrew. The implication is that there's one single, sacrosanct language through which we can communicate with God. By crossing that traditional line in the sand of semantics, Jesus swung wide the door for the New Testament to be written in Greek (instead of Hebrew) and ultimately be translated into thousands of other languages, dialects, and cultures so that millions and millions of people outside of Israel could hear and understand the message of God's unconditional love for mankind![49]

And the Lord's Prayer just keeps getting better because the very first word Jesus prays is *Abba,* the term a first-century Aramaic-speaking person would've called their earthly father, which in modern English would be "Dad" or "Papa." Most of the long-established synagogue renditions of the *Tefillah* (the Hebrew word for prayer) begin with: "God of Abraham, God of Isaac, and God of Jacob." A few others address the Creator of the Universe as "Holy One," "Mighty One," "Builder of Jerusalem," and "Redeemer of Israel." But get this: scholars find no evidence in pre-Christian Palestinian Judaism that God was ever addressed as *Abba* by an individual Jew in prayer prior to Jesus.[50] And the three additional times *abba* appears in the context of prayer in the New Testament (Mark 14:36, Rom. 8:15, and Gal. 4:6), the Greek expression *ho patēr*—which also means "Father"—is added so that in the original texts it reads: *Abba, ho patēr.* In effect: *Dad, Father.* This reiteration was surely necessary in a culture where regular folks could only access God through a priest in a highly structured religious system so the concept of addressing Him with an informal, affectionate, familial term of endearment like "Dad" would've been mind-blowing . . . if not heart-changing.

Kenneth Bailey shares a story in his book, *Jesus Through Middle Eastern Eyes,* about how the divine paternity revealed in Jesus's model prayer miraculously changed the heart of a young Latvian woman. Dr. Bailey met her at a Christian conference soon after the fall of the Soviet Union. Because he knew she'd been indoctrinated in atheism, he was curious about how she'd come to know Jesus. He inquired whether she had a family member who was a Christian or if she'd gone to an underground church or secret Bible study. All of which she responded no to. Then she told him this story:

> At funerals we were allowed to recite the Lord's Prayer. As a young child I heard those strange words and had no idea who we were talking to, what the words meant, where they came from or why we were reciting them. When freedom came at last, I had the opportunity to search for their meaning. When you are in total darkness, the tiniest point of light is very bright. For me the Lord's Prayer was that point of light. By the time I found its meaning, I was a Christian.[51]

The moment we put our trust and hope in Jesus Christ as our Savior, God's Spirit *abides* within us and around us. But since we can't see Him, sometimes we aren't conscious of His presence. Prayer is like pouring Miracle-Gro on our God-consciousness. Prayer—petitioning and praising God—helps us become more aware of His accessibility. And Jesus's model prayer assures us that we get to access our Creator-Redeemer in the natural context of relationship. Now that you think about it, fancy diction and decorum would seem just plain silly if they followed a "Dear Dad" salutation, wouldn't they?

- **HOW DO YOU** typically address God at the beginning of a prayer?

- **DO YOU USE** the same type of language when you're praying that you do in regular conversation? How about when you're praying in front of other people?

- **READ PSALM 116:2.** How could the imagery of God leaning down to listen to you affect the tone of your prayers?

Day 52

JESUS LOOSENS OUR GRIP ON STUFF

*Jesus said, "There was a certain rich man who was splendidly clothed in purple
and fine linen and who lived each day in luxury. At his gate lay a poor man named
Lazarus who was covered with sores. As Lazarus lay there longing for scraps
from the rich man's table, the dogs would come and lick his open sores.*

*"Finally, the poor man died and was carried by the angels to sit beside Abraham at the
heavenly banquet. The rich man also died and was buried, and he went to the place of the
dead. There, in torment, he saw Abraham in the far distance with Lazarus at his side.*

*"The rich man shouted, 'Father Abraham, have some pity! Send Lazarus over here to
dip the tip of his finger in water and cool my tongue. I am in anguish in these flames.'*

*"But Abraham said to him, 'Son, remember that during your lifetime you had
everything you wanted, and Lazarus had nothing. So now he is here being comforted,
and you are in anguish. And besides, there is a great chasm separating us. No one
can cross over to you from here, and no one can cross over to us from there.'*

*"Then the rich man said, 'Please, Father Abraham, at least send him to my father's home. For I
have five brothers, and I want him to warn them so they don't end up in this place of torment.'*

*"But Abraham said, 'Moses and the prophets have warned
them. Your brothers can read what they wrote.'*

*"The rich man replied, 'No, Father Abraham! But if someone is sent to them
from the dead, then they will repent of their sins and turn to God.'*

*"But Abraham said, 'If they won't listen to Moses and the prophets, they won't
be persuaded even if someone rises from the dead.'"* LUKE 16:19–31 NLT

I WAS STAYING AT a fancy hotel in downtown Dallas several years ago and
decided to squeeze in a quick workout before speaking at an event that evening.
By the time I'd finished pedaling and lifting and squatting, I was a dripping
mess. I toweled off as best I could and then hustled to the lobby elevator to
go back up to my room and get showered and changed for the shindig. The
elevator doors opened to reveal an impeccably dressed woman. And she was
dripping too, but with elegance instead of perspiration. Her suit was custom,
her jewelry was diamond-encrusted, and the alarmingly large pouf on top of
her head was perfect—not a hair out of place. Although it's a good thing I'm not

a smoker because, one spark, and surely her hairspray would've incinerated the both of us!

Since we were the only two people on the elevator and I noticed the button she'd already pressed was the number of the floor I was staying on too, I initiated a polite conversation by saying something about the weather. She stared straight ahead without any verbal or physical response, causing me to assume she was hard of hearing. So I leaned in a little closer and repeated my comment a whole lot louder. At which point, she glanced irritably out of the corner of her eye and exhaled loudly as if to say, "You are a stinky, sweaty, hot mess of a woman and I don't want *anything* to do with you." The next minute or so it took to reach our floor was awkward as I tried to feign fascination with the illuminated panel of floor buttons, and she rolled her eyes so many times it's a wonder they didn't get stuck that way.

An hour or so later, after I was showered, Spanxed, and suited up myself, I walked into the hotel banquet room that was filled with large donors of a national ministry and, lo and behold, guess who was there in all her condescending glory? When the program concluded and I was signing books in the lobby, she sashayed up to me with panache and gushed in a strong Southern drawl, "I wish you had told me who you were on the el-ah-vah-tah, I would've *loved* to chat with you had I known who you were." My natural inclination was to be offended, but God's Spirit reminded me to be kind because the truth was, she was the impoverished one. My heart softened when I thought how much love she had probably missed out on while locked away in her ivory tower.

The rich man and Lazarus is not an indictment about having too much money; it's an admonition to help those who don't have enough when you have extra. Contrary to some beliefs, our Savior did not preach socialism, but He did encourage stewardship. He consistently taught that while we're God's dearly loved children, He is the Creator and Sustainer of the universe and *we're tenants, not co-owners.* Because He loves us so much, He doesn't want us to be defined by our stuff and, therefore, vulnerable to being robbed. Robbed of peace and gratitude and rich relationships with people in different tax brackets. If your hope is balanced on a dime, you'll never really be secure.

- **ON A SCALE** of 1 to 10, with 1 being *consistently discontent* and 10 being *completely content*, how would you rate your level of satisfaction regarding your material possessions (place to live, furniture, car, clothing, etc.)?

- **WHILE JESUS ADVOCATED** *for* the monetarily poor, He didn't advocate *being* monetarily poor, as if poverty of possessions was the only road to spiritual maturity. Rather, He advocated for being poor in spirit, which simply means *humble,* no matter how much money you have! Why do you think so many Christians have an uneasy relationship with money?

- **READ HEBREWS 13:5.** How would you explain this to a teenager without sounding like a miser?

Day 53

JESUS IS OUR ONLY ATONEMENT

<u>For while we were still helpless, at the right time, Christ died for the ungodly.</u> For rarely will someone die for a just person—though for a good person perhaps someone might even dare to die. <u>But God proves his own love for us in that while we were still sinners, Christ died for us.</u> How much more then, since we have now been justified by his blood, will we be saved through him from wrath. For if, while we were enemies, we were reconciled to God through the death of his Son, then how much more, having been reconciled, will we be saved by his life. And not only that, but we also boast in God through our Lord Jesus Christ, through whom we have now received this reconciliation. ROMANS 5:6–11, EMPHASIS MINE

I THOROUGHLY ENJOYED WORKING as a lifeguard during the summers when I was in high school and college. I liked wearing a bathing suit to work, getting to work outside, and getting to meet all kinds of people. Furthermore, most of the "rescues" I performed weren't all that serious. I calmed down lots of panicked tourists who'd gotten in a tad over their head, had to shoo a juvenile gator out of the area a time or two so they wouldn't get near the swimmers, and once had the awkward task of getting a very large, very loud woman unstuck from her inner tube so, truth be told, Johnson's baby oil was the real hero that afternoon. But every now and then, I had the privilege of helping someone who was in serious trouble. And once, I almost went under myself while helping a would-be drowning victim.

It happened one Saturday when I was lifeguarding at a state park in Central Florida called Wekiva Springs, where the water is crystal clear and a constant seventy-two degrees—which can feel surprisingly cold on a ninety-five-plus degree Central Florida day. We typically had to make several rescues each weekend because, due to the clarity of the spring water, people often didn't realize how deep it was. And sometimes their energy ebbed before they were able to swim back to shallow water—which is exactly what happened to a woman that day. The minute I saw her flailing arms and bobbing head (right after I'd wolfed down the last bite of a chili cheese dog from the snack stand), I knew she was in trouble and immediately dove into the water to get her out.

When I reached her, I put her in a basic lifeguard hold and tried to calm her by assuring her she would be back on dry land in just a few minutes. I had pulled lots of big swimmers out of that deep area before, so I didn't think this petite dog-paddler would be any problem. But soon I was having a hard time keeping my head above water too. The woman was so much heavier than I expected. I strained with all my might, mentally chastising myself for scarfing down a chili-cheese dog while on the clock, and collapsed to the ground heaving with exhaustion (and processed pork nausea) when we finally made it back to shore. Which is when her husband—who, unbeknownst to me, had been hanging onto her legs the whole way—came sputtering up from the water behind her and began thanking me profusely for saving them both from drowning!

Much like my younger and leaner (despite inhaling copious amounts of chili cheese dogs) self in that red bathing suit, most people don't realize the weight of unconfessed sin they're lugging around. Because we're now living in an era where the majority of culture no longer frames its ethics by Judeo-Christian standards, the word *sin* now sounds like a relic in the museum of church history, leaving many ignorant of its life-threatening capacity. And you'll find no shortage of podcasts, books, and popular preachers who think it should remain hidden away in some dusty doctrinal corner because sin is a bitter, self-incriminating reality to chew on. Making it the theme of one's party guarantees most of the guests will leave early. However, without some comprehension of sin's gravity, it's impossible for us to appreciate the grace Jesus lavished on us through His atoning death on the cross.

Atonement is another word you rarely hear broadcasted these days either, but we should circulate a petition for its comeback because its meaning is glorious! In theological context, atonement refers to how Jesus Christ's substitutionary sacrifice satisfied the demands of God's just wrath upon sin. In other words, we were drowning, y'all—running out of breath, facing certain death and eternal separation from God—until the Messiah dove into the swirling waters of humanity to save us through His death on the cross. He died the death we deserved, on our behalf, so that we'd never have to taste death in eternity! And His wasn't a split-second decision either, because Peter explained our rescue had been God's plan all along: "Friends, I realize that what you and your leaders did to Jesus was done in ignorance. But God was fulfilling what all the prophets had foretold about the Messiah—that he *must* suffer these things" (Acts 3:17–18 NLT, emphasis mine).

Even though Jesus knew that loving us would lead to the cross, we've been on His mind before time began. Which takes a ton of weight off our prone-to-wander shoulders, doesn't it?

- **READ 1 JOHN 2:1-2.** How have you experienced this biblical truth personally?

- **READ GALATIANS 3:3.** How does your heart resonate with this verse? Does it provoke more guilt or gratitude?

- **RESEARCH THE PHRASE** "penal substitution." (If you've never heard it before, it may sound a tad tawdry, but I promise it isn't!) How would you restate this view of atonement to a child or a non-Christian?

Day 54
JESUS CHOSE TO BE A LEARNER

Every year his parents traveled to Jerusalem for the Passover Festival. When he was twelve years old, they went up according to the custom of the festival. After those days were over, as they were returning, the boy Jesus stayed behind in Jerusalem, but his parents did not know it. Assuming he was in the traveling party, they went a day's journey. Then they began looking for him among their relatives and friends. When they did not find him, they returned to Jerusalem to search for him. After three days, they found him in the temple sitting among the teachers, listening to them and asking them questions. And all those who heard him were astounded at his understanding and his answers. LUKE 2:41–47

WHEN MISSY WAS ABOUT six or seven years old, she asked me why Jesus had to die. I began to, once again, carefully explain how our disobedience causes us to be separated from the holiness of God—all the while inwardly berating myself that my daughter still didn't understand the Gospel even though I'm a Bible teacher by vocation! But Missy quickly interrupted me with this astute observation: "Mama, I know *why* Jesus had to die, I just want to know why God the Father picked His Son to be killed, because if one of us had to die, you wouldn't let it be me, you'd die so that I wouldn't have to." Her compelling question is one of the reasons I applied for a doctoral candidacy at Denver Seminary because it reminded me that I still have so many wonderful things left to learn in life. Studying our respective subjects while sitting side by side at the kitchen island has become one of my favorite parts of parenting. And I'm increasingly convinced that becoming a lifelong learner is more than just a pleasant pastime; it's an outgrowth of humility modeled by Christ Himself.

After camping in Jerusalem for a week or so and celebrating both Passover and the Feast of Unleavened Bread with friends and family, Joseph and Mary packed up the tent and began the long walk home to Galilee. Because caravans to and from the temple were normally made up of people from the same city or village,[52] Joseph and Mary assumed Jesus was somewhere amidst the crowd of dusty travelers as they hiked out of Jerusalem. They probably thought He was tossing a football around with some of His cousins. They didn't realize He was missing for an entire day.

I bet Mary's face was tense with worry on the trek back to Jerusalem to find her misplaced son. As soon as she and Joseph got to the edge of the Holy City, she pulled Jesus's middle school picture—the one that showed His cowlick and braces—out of her wallet and began asking everyone if they'd seen Him. She and Joseph anxiously knocked on doors, retraced their steps, and put flyers on windshields. By late afternoon they'd exhausted every lead and her mother's heart was heavy. She sat down wearily on a rock wall and began to weep.

Suddenly Joe leapt to his feet and cried, "Hey Mar—I'll bet He's at the temple because you know how much our boy *loves* school!" So they hurried across town, raced up the uneven temple steps two at a time, and burst into a classroom to finally find their son sitting cross-legged on the floor discussing theology with a group of dumbfounded men five and six times His age!

If I was the smartest person in the world, I'd want at least a few people to be impressed. Not that I would necessarily post my academic stats on social media, but I probably wouldn't mind if someone else did! Thank heaven, Jesus is nothing like me and didn't feel the need to flaunt His unprecedented brainpower:

> But they did not understand what he said to them.
> Then he went down with them and came to Nazareth and was obedient to them. His mother kept all these things in her heart. And Jesus increased in wisdom and stature, and in favor with God and with people. (Luke 2:50–52, emphasis mine)

In other words, although Jesus was infinitely smarter than His parents—*who did not understand what He said to them*—He still submitted to them. According to Luke's account (which Mary probably described to him[53]), Jesus got up, followed His confused parents back home to Nazareth, and continued acquiescing to their altogether ordinary authority. And while Jesus likely understood His divine calling and identity before He even started shaving, He didn't groan when Mary mispronounced a big word, and He didn't try to tutor Joseph in the physics of carpentry and construction. Nor should we forget that as Mary and Joe's beloved firstborn son, the Master of the Universe condescended to master the art of rolling over, then crawling, and ultimately walking and talking like a normal child. Our Redeemer has always been omniscient—His beautiful mind contains the wisdom of the ages—yet He humbly chose to engage in His incarnate life as a learner.

- **READ HEBREWS 5:8.** What have you *learned* through suffering? Have you learned/grown spiritually more during easy seasons (when most of the relationships in your life are free from contention and things are going smoothly) or during difficult, suffering kind of seasons?

- **READ PSALM 139:1-4,** Job 21:22, and Hebrews 4:13. What's the main point these verses make about God's "mind"?

- **READ ROMANS 11:33-36.** How has being mentally awed by who God is led to worship in your own life?

Day 55

JESUS SMILES

"When he has found it, <u>he joyfully</u> puts it on his shoulders, and coming home, he calls his friends and neighbors together, saying to them, 'Rejoice with me, because I have found my lost sheep!' I tell you, in the same way, <u>there will be more joy in heaven</u> over one sinner who repents than over ninety-nine righteous people who don't need repentance." LUKE 15:5–7, EMPHASIS MINE

"I have told you these things so that <u>my joy may be in you</u> and your joy may be complete." JOHN 15:11, EMPHASIS MINE

MY PRECIOUS MOM, PATTI Angel (yes, that really is her last name!), who introduced me to Jesus, is eighty-five years young and is a wonderful example of the ever-increasing joy and liberty that should define Christ-followers. She comes up to Tennessee from Florida several months out of the year to spend time with us, and during one of her recent winter visits we had a blast playing games by the fire, staying up late telling stories, and schlepping through the early January snow that blanketed our five-acre "farmette." Mom even good-naturedly wedged her wee self on a sled with my nephew, John Michael, and belly laughed with glee while barreling down a steep slope on the backside of our property!

I don't have many childhood memories that include that kind of liberated happiness with Mom. Because she'd been taught by several spiritual leaders that being a "good Christian" was more about what you *couldn't* do than what you could. And undomesticated delight was on the naughty list. Before I learned how to read, I'd learned to regard that big, black, leather-bound King James edition—which stood on the most prominent shelf in our living room—as a *supremely sober book.* And while it indeed holds parts that sober us up about certain things, it took a long time to unlearn my initial wariness about the overall love story we call the Bible and to see Jesus (the undisputed Hero of this oh-so-important book) as a *smiling* Savior, not some sour-faced kind of chaperon trying to suck all the fun out of life.

When I was Missy's age, I admired how my mother carried herself with polished poise and often thought: *I hope one day I'll be as beautiful as her.* I had a similar thought recently while watching Mom and Missy with their heads bent together, giggling conspiratorially about something they thought was especially funny. Now when I watch Mom, I find myself hoping to one day have a heart that's as beautifully bent toward God and others as hers. Because the decades of following God—even when she unwittingly stumbled down paths He hadn't paved—have weathered her soul into the gorgeous patina of a joyful woman who can laugh at the days to come (Prov. 31:25).

While there's no single verse proving that our Savior smiled or laughed during His earthly life and ministry, there are a plethora of passages that imply His good humor, like the times He cracked jokes. Or consider Genesis 1:26–27, which reveals that humans are made in God's image, and since most of us love to laugh, He probably does too! Furthermore, many of the stories Jesus told contain a light-hearted literary wink, such as when He used intentional hyperbole like: having "a log in your eye while noticing a neighbor's splinter" (Matt. 7:3–5), or "a giant mammal of a camel attempting to squeeze through the minuscule eye of a needle" (Matt. 19:24). In addition, Jesus promised that mirth would follow mourning in the Beatitudes: "God blesses you who weep now, for in due time *you will laugh*" (Luke 6:21b NLT, emphasis mine).

And let's take a moment to consider how the Pharisees accused Jesus of being a frivolous friend and partier: "The Son of Man has come eating and drinking, and you say, 'Look, a glutton and a drunkard, a friend of tax collectors and sinners!'" (Luke 7:34), which certainly wouldn't have crossed their lips if they'd only seen His somber side, right? Finally, Jesus shirked off the formality of a first-century rabbi and bear-hugged kids—likely sticky from eating candy and clamoring for His attention like puppies:

> One day some parents brought their children to Jesus so he could touch and bless them. But the disciples scolded the parents for bothering him.
>
> When Jesus saw what was happening, he was angry with his disciples. He said to them, "Let the children come to me. Don't stop them! For the Kingdom of God belongs to those who are like these children. I tell you the truth, anyone who doesn't receive the Kingdom of God like a child will never enter it." Then he took the children in his arms and placed his hands on their heads and blessed them. (Mark 10:13–16 NLT)

Children aren't drawn to unsmiling grumps and, come to think of it, most adults aren't either. Therefore, if we want to reflect some measure of the grace God has lavished upon us, let's all agree to smile more often and regard belly laughs as short bursts of praise for our Savior's glory!

- **READ PSALM 40:16.** On a scale of 1 to 10, with 1 being *not at all* and 10 being *right on the button*, how well does this verse describe you?

- **READ NUMBERS 6:24–26 (NLT),** Proverbs 16:15 (NLT), and Psalm 80 (CEV). Are you more comfortable picturing our Creator-Redeemer with a smiling countenance or a serious countenance? Why do you think that is?

- **READ MATTHEW 3:17.** How would you paraphrase God's response after Johnny B baptized Jesus?

Day 56

JESUS IS THE FINAL AND FULL WORD OF GOD

For the word of God is alive and active. Sharper than any double-edged sword, it penetrates even to dividing soul and spirit, joints and marrow; it judges the thoughts and attitudes of the heart. HEBREWS 4:12 NIV

HI, MY NAME IS Lisa and I'm also a recovering Bible swinger. Here's the deal: when I was growing up in church, the more engaging youth pastors I listened to used lots of volume while preaching and most of them swung great big Bibles around like Olympic hammer throwers when they were emphasizing pejorative points like: *if you sip an alcoholic beverage, you'll become intoxicated, which leads to hell*; or *if you skip youth group for a day at the beach, you'll become backslidden, which leads to hell*; or *if you engage in HEAVY PETTING, you'll become inflamed with lust, which leads to hell.* Which by the way, this propelled me to run crying to the altar and confess my presumed sin at a youth conference when I was in middle school because I innocently thought the speaker was referring to rubbing your pet too hard and I was afraid I might've used a little too much pressure when stroking the fur of our sweet mutt Smokey after sampling Mountain Dew for the first time with my cousin. But that's another story for another devotion.

Anyway, based on my early experience with spiritual leaders who gestured passionately with their leather-bound "swords," I eventually drew the conclusion that gesturing passionately *with* a Bible while teaching *from* the Bible was required behavior for anyone who wanted to be an effective communicator of the Gospel. Which I instantly regretted one evening early in my career when I was the guest speaker at a "Women in the Word" event held in a lovely little Baptist church. I had gotten all worked up about a passage, and when I swung the personally engraved, NIV translation of Holy Writ that my mom gave me for Christmas when I was a senior in high school, the entire book of Genesis ripped free from the binding, shot over the altar, and struck an elderly woman on the front pew right in the chest.

My hope is that none of you have succumbed to any unnecessary Bible hurling, but my guess is that some of you could still use some realignment when it comes to handling God's enscripturated Word, so let's start with an old-fashioned "sword drill":

The Word of God is sharper than a _____ .

If you said: *a double-edged sword,* you hit it right on the chest, ahem, I mean nose!

As for your answer for the last question, what specific verse did you derive your answer from? (book, chapter, and verse?)

_____

If you said: *Hebrews 4:12,* you are two-for-two!

What's the overarching theme of the book of Hebrews?

If you said: *the superiority of Jesus Christ to the Old Covenant and the sole sufficiency of His atonement for our salvation,* you are cooking with gas, baby!

Who was the original audience that Hebrews was preached to before it was inscribed as an epistle?

If you said: *first-century Jewish believers who were seriously considering apostacy because of the widespread oppression, abuse, and martyrdom they were experiencing in their polytheistic, largely pagan culture that was led by megalomaniac emperors who were paranoid about the possibility that Christianity could usurp their absolute power and control,* you have hereby earned a pass from volunteering in the church nursery for at least a month!

When was Hebrews written?

If you said: *between AD 60–70, and it couldn't have been later than AD 70 because that's when the temple was destroyed, which is featured prominently in the text,* your name will be shouted from small group rooftops!

And does anyone have a clue when the Bible as we know it—with both Old and New Testaments—was canonized?

If you said: *the first unofficial canon of New Testament Scripture was compiled by Marcion of Sinope around AD 140, but the first comprehensive and official canon of the Christian Bible didn't exist until Athanasius compiled it in the fourth century, and it wasn't formally canonized until the councils of Hippo and Carthage in AD 393 and AD 419,* I will personally come to your house and rub your feet!

Here's the point I'm trying to make, y'all—the author of Hebrews wasn't simply talking about a leather-bound Bible when he preached that the "word of God" was living and active and sharper than a two-edged sword because the Christian Bible as we know it didn't even exist back then! However, the original Greek word—*logos*—that's translated "word of God" in Hebrews 4, is the exact same word used to describe Jesus in John 1, so in light of the historical context of Hebrews, chapter 4 verse 12 must be referring to the resurrected Messiah! The Word of God made flesh! Jesus is *alive and active.* He is *sharper than any double-edged sword, able to penetrate even to dividing soul and spirit, joints and marrow!* He is the one able to *judge the thoughts and attitudes of our hearts.* And the fact that Jesus is the main subject here in Hebrews becomes all the more evident in light of the following verse: "No creature is hidden from him, but all things are naked and exposed to the eyes of *him* to whom we must give an account" (v. 13, emphasis mine).

It goes without saying that the supernatural "melding" of the Bible and Jesus is a mystery that's impossible to wrap our finite minds around. God *chose* enscripturated revelation as the *main* means through which to point humanity toward our Redeemer. He could've written His will in the sky with stardust; instead, He spelled it out in a sacred, readable *Book of Life.* But the thief on the cross didn't have any Bible verses to quote in those last moments of life to justify himself; he only had a brand-new faith in a flesh-and-blood Messiah, the *Word of God* he was being crucified alongside. Yet his brief encounter and subsequent belief in Jesus was enough for him to gain entrance to Glory (Luke 23:43). Therefore, I think it's important for passionate Bible bangers and would-be Bible swingers to recognize that sometimes the phrase "Word of God" in the New Testament refers to Jesus. For instance, when Paul tells Timothy to "preach the word" (2 Tim. 4:2), he's not talking about expository preaching, he's encouraging young Tim to keep Jesus at the center of every message he shares!

Frankly, I think one of the reasons we have such a high rate of biblical illiteracy among believers today is that we've segregated Jesus—*Logos*—from our leather-bound copies of God's promises and parameters. But the good news is that when we stop framing the Word of God as merely truthful data to wrap our ethics around and begin to connect it to the work and person of *JESUS CHRIST,* we'll quit beating people up with it and will become increasingly convinced that He loves us *and* them!

- **ONE OF MY** seminary professors, Dr. Don Payne, says: "If we think of Scripture primarily as an instruction manual, things are going to get toxic really quickly!" How would you synopsize his statement?

- **WAS YOUR FIRST** experience with the Bible more promissory or punitive?

- **WHEN YOU HAVE** a chunk of free time this week, marinate in Psalm 119. What lyrics about God's precepts—His enscripturated promises and parameters—resonate most deeply with you?

Day 57
JESUS KNOWS WHERE HIS HOME IS

But you are a chosen race, a royal priesthood, a holy nation, a people for his possession, so that you may proclaim the praises of the one who called you out of darkness into his marvelous light. <u>Once you were not a people, but now you are God's people</u>; you had not received mercy, but now you have received mercy.

Dear friends, I urge you <u>as strangers and exiles</u> to abstain from sinful desires that wage war against the soul. 1 PETER 2:9–11, EMPHASIS MINE

———

THREE YEARS AGO, I got to take Missy on an African safari and it was like a dream come true for me because I've loved that continent since I was about seven years old and we had a missionary from Africa stay in our house. Which means that for fifty years I romanticized the idea of camping out in the wilds of Africa. So, you can probably imagine my jet-lagged delight when Missy and I arrived in South Africa—after thirty-seven hours of travel—and the manager of the resort cheerfully informed me that she'd upgraded our booking to a private lodge on a bluff overlooking a river where wild game were guaranteed to gather at sunrise and sunset.

What she didn't tell me was that our lodge was located several miles into the bush, so we had to be escorted there by two guides with automatic rifles to protect us en route because of the lions and other big cats. It wasn't until after those same guides had thoroughly swept our lodge making sure it was animal-free, checked the locks on every window and door, warned me not to open any of those same doors or windows until they came to fetch us the following morning, and were waving goodbye, that they mentioned seeing an eight-foot black mamba right outside our "luxury lodge" earlier that day, which is why they swept the premises so thoroughly.

Then they zoomed off in their Land Rover before I had a chance to faint. Because I'd spent much of our thirty-seven-hour trek to Africa reading up on the wild animals we might encounter on safari and knew that black mambas are one of the fastest, most venomous snakes in the world that can grow up to fourteen feet long. Two drops of their venom can kill a person. Plus, it's imperative not to look directly at or move toward a mamba because they interpret that as aggression and will usually respond by attacking, oftentimes launching themselves through the air toward their victim before sinking their fangs into said victim's flesh.

I tried to remain calm while getting Missy settled into the beautiful mosquito-netted bed, then I began praying out loud while unpacking our suitcases and getting myself ready for bed. But when I turned out the lights and heard a persistent thump-shuffle-thump sound in the pitch-black darkness of our remote lodge miles away from another human, I felt my pulse quicken. By the time I found the remote to turn on the lights, the sound had gotten much louder and I realized it was coming from *inside a tall woven basket in the corner of the bedroom* that looked exactly like those baskets snake-charmers keep cobras in. I quickly picked up the phone to call the main lodge, only to find out there was no connection and, of course, there was no cell service.

My mind was racing, trying to figure out how to deal with what I was sure was a coiled mamba getting ready to launch itself at us because we obviously couldn't hike two miles back to the main lodge in the dark with predators roaming all around us and there was no way to call for help. So I began rooting around for some kind of weapon, while keeping an eye on the swaying hamper, but the only thing I could find was an umbrella. I grabbed it and began tiptoeing stealthily toward the mystery creature, determined to save my child. Unfortunately, when I "hooked" the top of the basket to keep it from dumping the snake out on the floor, a big hairy critter that looked like a cross between a kangaroo and a bug-eyed rat came flying out with a loud shriek.

I didn't have time to feel relief that it wasn't a mamba because that huge roo-rat began shrieking and racing across the curtain rods around the room, and since I didn't know whether it was poisonous or carnivorous, I started chasing it, swinging the umbrella like a sword, which caused it to panic and spray urine like some kind of marsupial mace. It probably only took three or four minutes of flailing to herd it out of the sliding glass doors, but it felt like hours. I slumped on the floor afterwards and had to focus to keep from hyperventilating. I finally got back in bed—taking the umbrella with me—but, of course, didn't sleep a wink because jousting with that crazed vermin (I found out later the intruder was a giant galago, which are *louder* than they are dangerous) jerked me back into the reality that we were no longer in the safe familiarity of our beloved Tennessee hills; we were in the wilds of *Africa*!

Hopefully it won't take a thirty-seven-hour three-plane journey and a screeching intruder to remind you that, as a Christ-follower, you're no longer at home either. In fact, Hebrews 11:13 describes those of us who've put our hope in Jesus as "foreigners and temporary residents on the earth," which is reminiscent of how Jesus describes Himself: "Jesus told him, 'Foxes have dens, and birds of the sky have nests, but the Son of Man has no place to lay his head'" (Matt. 8:20). Keep in mind, this verse follows our Savior's assurance in Matthew 6 that our heavenly Father will care for His children better than He did for the birds and the flowers (vv. 25–34).[54] So it's less about becoming literally destitute or transient than it is about making sure *our home is in Him.* Said another way, Jesus knew where His true home was, and so should we. Jesus and us, we are temporary citizens in this fallen world, our real home being the new heavens and new earth—the recreated, regenerated world that awaits us on the other side of resurrection. Our true home is with Jesus in a world set right again.

The truth is we're probably going to stick out like sore thumbs and fifth wheels in the company of family, friends, and coworkers who haven't met Jesus yet and are happy as clams in this fallen world. But if we live like Jesus lived—showing others that we don't need the temporary comforts that a world disrupted by sin can offer (which are actually meager offerings in the scheme of things!)—we can help those around us remember there's a truer and better home, and Father of that home, awaiting us all!

- **IN WHAT WAYS** is it obvious to you that this world is fallen? Asked another way, what parts of this fallen life often cause you to either mourn or long for the world to come?

- **ON THE FLIP** side, what ways have you perhaps grown too comfortable or complacent in this fallen world? Asked another way, what parts of this life tempt you to not only forget, but lose your longing for that recreated, regenerated world that lies on the other side of this one?

- **READ 2 CORINTHIANS 5:17.** What shifted in you after you put your hope in Jesus? What "old thing" doesn't show up in your heart, mind, and actions anymore?

Day 58

JESUS IS INFINITELY PATIENT
WITH OUR ALL-TOO-HUMANNESS

Immediately he made the disciples get into the boat and go ahead of him to the other side, while he dismissed the crowds. After dismissing the crowds, he went up on the mountain by himself to pray. Well into the night, he was there alone. Meanwhile, the boat was already some distance from land, battered by the waves, because the wind was against them. Jesus came toward them walking on the sea very early in the morning. When the disciples saw him walking on the sea, they were terrified. "It's a ghost!" they said, and they cried out in fear.

Immediately Jesus spoke to them. "Have courage! It is I. Don't be afraid."

"Lord, if it's you," Peter answered him, "command me to come to you on the water."

He said, "Come."

And climbing out of the boat, Peter started walking on the water and came toward Jesus. But when he saw the strength of the wind, he was afraid, and beginning to sink he cried out, "Lord, save me!"

Immediately Jesus reached out his hand, caught hold of him, and said to him, "You of little faith, why did you doubt?" MATTHEW 14:22–31

THE FIRST FEW HOURS in the hospital were scary. Especially after I overheard two of the medical personnel who were hovering around me discuss how my particular case of COVID had caused the excess fluid in my lungs to harden and crystalize like shards of glass. One said wearily, "Based on how shredded her lungs are from the scans, I'm not sure we'll be able to stabilize her." In defense of those health-care workers who were risking their own lives in a selfless attempt to save mine, I was so weak I could only lay there with my eyes closed, so I'm sure they thought I was unconscious and unable to hear their conversation.

It was still disconcerting though. I've participated in extreme sports like jumping mountain bikes off small cliffs, skiing and snowboarding down double black diamonds, parasailing in high winds, scuba diving around sharks, running with bulls, and operating a chainsaw, so there've been a few times I realized in retrospect that my life may've been in danger. But I've never been lying on a hospital bed while entertaining that idea.

Fortunately, my first thought was the promise I got to preach at my Dad Angel's funeral, eight weeks after he'd put his faith in Jesus: absent from the body, present with the Lord (2 Cor. 5:8). I can clearly remember thinking: Oh my goodness, this is what peace with God feels like! Any minute now, I'm going to come up out of this wheezing jar of clay and walk right into the waiting arms of Jesus! Then, after maybe a whopping thirty seconds of rock-solid faith, my mind came screeching to an all-too-human thought and I panicked at the thought of Missy losing another mom. I began silently begging God not to let me die until she was at least eighteen because I couldn't bear the thought of her being orphaned all over again.

I should've known better, y'all. I've been walking with God for more than fifty years now, and I know He's not cruel. Plus, I believe His absolute sovereignty is always woven with mercy. That even if we can't see it in the natural, ultimately "in *all things* God works for the good of those who love him, who have been called according to his purpose" (Rom. 8:28 NIV, emphasis mine). But in that moment, all the theological reasoning and memory verses in my heart and mind retreated, and what I was left with was gripping anxiety about my daughter's well-being.

I thought I deserved a lecture for being even weaker spiritually than I was physically. Instead, the presence of Christ filled the room and suddenly all that reverberated in my hard head was, in essence, *Honey, I've got her. I love her more than you and I will never leave her. Whether you live or die, I will love and take care of both of you forever.* The resounding, supernatural comfort and nearness of our Savior was so gentle and kind that I felt my whole body relax in response. His patience with my fallenness saturated me with a peace like I'd never known before.

I've heard the passage about Peter getting out of the boat in an attempt to walk on water toward Jesus countless times. And the focus of the sermon or lesson is usually one of two things; either it's about how Peter at least *tried* to show his loyalty to Jesus by getting out of the boat (unlike the other disciples), or it's about how his immature faith caused him to forget the supremacy of Jesus in the face of really big waves. And both are true. Pete did exhibit a sliver of faith and he did wobble like a toddler with a weighted diaper.

However, what jumps out to me lately in the passage is how Jesus beckons him: *Come.* The command in this scene, to me, sounds like how patient parents talk when teaching their toddler to walk—knowing the knees of their child's faith will buckle, allowing him to fall, and understanding he'll need help to get back up again. If we were to graph Peter's faith-walk during the three years he spent by Jesus's side (and would continue to be the ongoing rhythm of his gait), we'd probably chart it this way: *wobble, fall, and get back up again; wobble, fall, and get back up again; wobble, fall, and get back up again.* Yet Jesus never gave up on Pete. He just kept picking him up, giving him an affectionate pat on the back, and encouraging him to work on being a dependable disciple. Until Pete finally learned to stride in such steadfast devotion that when he was ultimately martyred for following Jesus, he asked to be crucified upside down because he humbly refused to die in the same posture as His Lord.

I can so identify with Peter's cry of desperation: *Lord, save me!* And I hope one day to mirror his eventual steadfast devotion after a lifetime of walking with our Savior. Until then, I will remain grateful that Jesus still picks me up when I fall. And I pray you will too.

- **THE WORD *PATIENCE*** in the New Testament comes from two Greek root words: *makros*, which means "long," and *thymia*, which means "feeling." In other words, patience is having control of one's feelings for a long period of time.[55] Who best exemplifies that in your circle of family and friends?

- **READ ROMANS 2:4.** How did you experience God's patience before you put your hope in Jesus?

- **READ COLOSSIANS 3:12–13.** How can these verses help you extend patience toward the bumbling slow learners in your little corner of the world?

Day 59
JESUS HAS EIGHT BILLION FAVORITES

As he was teaching in one of the synagogues on the Sabbath, a woman was there who had been disabled by a spirit for over eighteen years. She was bent over and could not straighten up at all. When Jesus saw her, he called out to her, "Woman, you are free of your disability." Then he laid his hands on her, and instantly she was restored and began to glorify God. LUKE 13:10–13

See what great love the Father has given us that we should be called God's children—and we are! 1 JOHN 3:1A

ONE MORNING, AT THE very beginning of yet another great but grueling day in a doctoral class at Denver Seminary, I was startled when my professor grabbed the front of my desk and asked me to look directly into his eyes. At first, I thought I was in trouble, but the twinkle in his eyes told me that wasn't the case. After a long moment of smiling at me, he said slowly and sincerely, "Lisa, *you* are God's favorite." Then he just kept staring at me with this huge grin. Eleven of my peers were now watching the encounter with unbridled curiosity, so I was slightly mortified that Dr. Strait had chosen to single me out as a teacher's pet. It was all I could do not to chuckle with embarrassment and mumble something dismissive to break what was beginning to feel like polite tension.

Just before I was tempted to scoot my chair away from him, Dr. Strait stepped sideways and did the exact same thing to the student sitting next to me. And on it went until he'd told all twelve of us that *we* were God's favorite. Then he opened the syllabus and happily announced: "Let's talk about the infinite nature of Jesus!" He then went on to explain how our Savior's unconditional love cannot dissipate. Unlike our experience in human relationships (which in their limited nature, have capacity thresholds), when Jesus gives you what feels to be an extraordinarily large slice of His attention and affection, it doesn't mean that someone else gets a smaller piece of proverbial pie. Unlike us, Jesus doesn't run out of emotional energy. Nor does He prefer honor students to remedial ones. Or healthy kids to sick ones.

There's several interesting details in the story of the bent-over woman that aren't immediately apparent in the text, and one is that this is the last recorded time that Jesus taught in a synagogue before the crucifixion and resurrection. So this is effectively our Savior's swan song. It's His last public sermon. It's the final number of His farewell tour. And the original Greek text from which we get the English translation "When Jesus saw her" (v. 12) indicates that she surprised Jesus. That she wasn't present on a back pew at the beginning of His message but actually interrupted it, in addition to breaking the "testosterone only" rule that applied to whenever Torah was being taught in the sanctuary. Seems like that would've been more than enough to get her kicked off His list of favorites, right?

She was evidently so sick and tired of being sick and tired that she didn't care about protocol anymore. New Testament scholars propose she was suffering from either a serious case of spinal stenosis or kyphosis, and since some translations describe her as "bent double," this woman obviously had a very painful curvature of the spine. She couldn't sit comfortably in a chair. Or pick up her kids. Or lie on her back. Or see beyond a few feet in front of her. So it makes sense that her desperation would drive her to seek the help of a rabbi with a reputation for healing.

However, His response defies human logic because He stops right there in the middle of exegeting the Old Testament to a bunch of stuffy dudes and calls out to her. Then He steps down from the platform, strides down the aisle toward her, and envelops her in a healing hug. Even though Jesus was busy and she was broken, she didn't *bother* Him—He welcomed the interruption!

I think some of us stay bent because we don't want to be a bother. So we swallow our pain and paste on plastic smiles and try to be "good" for Jesus's sake. But y'all, we can't be a bother to Jesus because (1) He has more than enough attention to go around, and (2) we're His *BRIDE*! And every single one of our eight billion breathing selves on this spinning planet called Earth can legitimately lay claim to the fact that we're His favorite—all it takes is asking for His help like that bent-over woman. If you've never done so, it goes something like this:

Dear Jesus, I'm a hot mess.
I've made a lot of mistakes that have sep-
arated me from God's holiness.
And a lot of mistakes have been made against
me that have broken my heart.
So I need Your forgiveness and Your healing.
I believe that You're the only One who can save me.
I believe You came to this earth; lived a perfect, sinless
life; shed your blood on a cross on humanity's behalf;
and were raised from the dead after three days.
I'm putting all my hope and faith in those facts.
Here's my whole heart, Jesus; it's Yours now.
Thank You for forgiving me and loving me unconditionally.
Help me to rest in Your grace and live the
rest of my life to make You smile.
Amen.

- **REREAD 1 JOHN 3:1A.** Have you ever honestly felt lavished by God's love? If not, have you asked to be?

- **READ SONG OF SONGS 4:9.** If you could actually see Jesus right now with your natural eyesight and He was telling you how you captured His heart with one glance, could you meet His gaze? Why or why not?

- **TURN TO PSALM 139** in your Bible (it's right around the middle), and if you're comfortable writing in it, inscribe your name over every pronoun so as to personalize it. Then read the first seventeen verses with your name inserted. How does your heart respond?

Day 60

JESUS IS EVERYTHING

God, you are my God; I eagerly seek you.
I thirst for you;
my body faints for you
in a land that is dry, desolate, and without water.
So I gaze on you in the sanctuary
to see your strength and your glory.

My lips will glorify you
because <u>your faithful love is better than life.</u>
PSALM 63:1–3, EMPHASIS MINE

Who do I have in heaven but you?
And I desire nothing on earth but you.

My flesh and my heart may fail,
but <u>God is the strength of my heart,</u>
<u>my portion forever.</u>
PSALM 73:25–26, EMPHASIS MINE

But I consider my life of no value to myself; <u>my purpose is to finish</u>
<u>my course and the ministry I received from the Lord Jesus, to testify</u>
<u>to the gospel of God's grace.</u> ACTS 20:24, EMPHASIS MINE

More than that, <u>I also consider everything to be a loss in view of the surpassing</u>
<u>value of knowing Christ Jesus my Lord.</u> PHILIPPIANS 3:8A, EMPHASIS MINE

ON APRIL 14, 2014, I woke Missy up from a twin cot in a Haitian orphanage and bundled her into a van I'd rented for our trip to the Port-au-Prince airport. I couldn't quite believe that our roller coaster of a two-year adoption journey was coming to an end, and I was getting to bring her home. I soon found myself holding my breath and glancing anxiously at the clock in the gate area of the airport every few minutes, half expecting someone to come up and try to pry her from my arms after all the trauma we'd been through. It took restraint not to run when an American Airlines agent opened the boarding door.

Two hours later, Missy was happily preoccupied with a cartoon on my iPad when we landed in Miami, and didn't notice the tears rolling down my face. I had to wipe more away as we inched our way through the customs line holding hands, because reality was beginning to sink in that after twenty-four months of slogging through seemingly endless paperwork, the maddeningly slow Haitian child welfare system, and worrying about her physical and emotional health from two thousand miles away, the dream God set in my heart when I was seventeen years old was finally coming true.

My heart had claimed her the first time I held her in April 2012, when she was covered in scabies, her little lungs filled with fluid from tuberculosis, her body frail from malnutrition, her hair reddened by the lack of nutrients in what scarce amounts of food she was getting, and her baby teeth brown from lack of care and clean water. After getting to spend that first week with that beautiful baby, I'd memorized the way her eyelids got heavy during her favorite bedtime lullabies, the way she wiggled when she was excited, and the fierce resolve in her eyes when she was determined. It just took two long years to get the official documents proving what my heart had known all along: I was meant to be her second mama.

By the time we got to Nashville, we were both worn out but then buoyed by all the thoughtful well-wishers waiting for us at the airport. Several of my dear friends and their husbands escorted us out to my car—all the while singing Missy's favorite songs, much to her delight—and after a sweet prayer and group hugs, I buckled my smiling child into the brand-new car seat I'd broken several nails installing the week before. Then, almost as soon as we began the forty-five-minute drive home, the sky opened up and it began pouring rain.

I was so focused on navigating through rush hour traffic in the storm, and the thunder and lightning were so loud, that it took me a minute to realize Missy had started crying. Poor little thing, all the emotions from our Gotcha Day had finally gotten too heavy for her four-year-old shoulders to bear. The driving conditions were so bad that I couldn't take my eyes off the road, so I tried to sooth her by speaking in Creole, telling her how much I loved her, and that everything would be alright, but her sobs only got more desperate.

Since an exit was still miles away, the only thing I could think to do was reach my right hand back between the gap in the front seats in a last-ditch effort to comfort her until I could manage to get off the interstate. Almost immediately I felt the warm grasp of her tiny hand in mine, and we traveled like that—blindly holding hands through a ferocious storm—until I was able to pull off the road into a gas station and climb in the back seat with her to hold her while she got her bearings.

And we did that—held hands through the gap in the front car seats—almost every day from April 14, 2014, until Missy got big enough to ride up front with me. Now most days on the way to or from school, she reaches for my hand over the middle console.

It's a wonder God has trusted me with any love at all this side of Glory because I was so afraid of losing it that I spent years subconsciously running from it. Consequently, I've never been married, so I don't know what self-sacrificing romantic love feels like. But we had the joy of attending a friend's wedding recently and my heart stood up and stretched its slow-to-develop shoulders wide when Missy reached for my hand during their vows. Then—after we'd held up sparklers and watched the new, deliriously happy couple get into a chauffeured Mercedes and drive off for the reception—she squeezed my hand and said sincerely, "Mom, I don't love you like they love each other, but I'll still love you until the death-do-us-part part." And I thought: "Surely, this is in some small part what the psalmist was expressing about Jesus when he sang: 'And when I awake in heaven, *I will be fully satisfied*, for I will see you face-to-face'" (Ps. 17:15b TLB, emphasis mine).

My heart exults over my daughter, who is God's second greatest gift to me. But Jesus is my *everything*.

There is none like You
No one else can touch my heart like You do
And I can search for all eternity, Lord
And find, there is none like You.[56]

- **IS JESUS YOUR** *everything*? If not, what could you change to give Him the lion's share of your heart?

NOTES

1. J. I. Packer, *Knowing God* (Downers Grove, IL: InterVarsity Press, 1973), 53.

2. Don Payne, "Biblical and Theological Reflection on the Practice of Ministry," Class Lecture Notes, Denver Seminary, July 2019.3.

3. Packer, *Knowing God*, 53.

4. Please forgive me the intentional grammatical error of not capitalizing that lying lizard's name, even though "enemy" or "satan" are technically proper pronouns!

5. Robert H. Stein, *The Method and Message of Jesus's Teachings* (Louisville, KY: Westminster John Knox Press, 1994), 4–5.

6. Timothy Keller, *Jesus the King* (New York: Penguin Books, 2016), 227.

7. Keller, *Jesus the King*, 227.

8. Donna B. Stinnett, "Nazareth's Rich History Places Visitors in Footsteps of Jesus," *GoSanAngelo,* December 21, 2013, https://archive.gosanangelo.com/lifestyle/nazareths-rich-history-places-visitors-in-footsteps-of-jesus-ep-305779993-355218701.html/.

9. William Hendriksen, *New Testament Commentary: Exposition of the Gospel According to Luke* (Grand Rapids, MI: Baker Book House, 1996), 255.

10. Gerhard F. Hasel, "Sabbath," ed. David Noel Freedman, *The Anchor Yale Bible Dictionary* (New York: Doubleday, 1992), 849.

11. https://www.asor.org/anetoday/2016/01/crime-and-punishment-in-pharaonic-egypt/#:~:text=Corporal%20punishments%20consisted%20of%20beatings,mutilation%20of%20nose%20and%20ears

12. James Dobson, *Coming Home: Timeless Wisdom for Families* (Wheaton, IL: Tyndale House Publishers, 1998), 194–95.

13. https://www.chabad.org/library/article_cdo/aid/112333/jewish/Nimrod-and-Abraham.htm

14. F. L. Cross and Elizabeth A. Livingstone, eds., *The Oxford Dictionary of the Christian Church* (Oxford; New York: Oxford University Press, 2005), 1,724.

15. Craig Blomberg, *Interpreting the Parables* (Downers Grove, IL: InterVarsity Press; 2012), 447–49.

16. Blomberg, *Interpreting the Parables*, 447–49.

17. Taken from John Ortberg's message, *Was Christianity Opposed to Women?*, http://www.johnortberg.com.

18. Ortberg's message, *Was Christianity Opposed to Women?*

19. Flavius Josephus, *Against Apion*, 2.201.

20. *Dictionary of Jesus and the Gospels*, eds. J. B. Green, S. McKnight, and I. H. Marshall (Downers Grove, IL: InterVarsity Press, 1992), 880.

21. J. Julius Scott Jr., *Jewish Backgrounds of the New Testament* (Grand Rapids, MI: Baker Book House, 1995), 248–49.

22. *ESV Study Bible (The Holy Bible, English Standard Version)* (Wheaton, IL: Crossway, 1967).

23. Barbara Johnson, *Boomerang Joy: Joy That Goes Around, Comes Around* (Grand Rapids, MI: Zondervan, 2000), 167.

24. Robert James Utley, *The Beloved Disciple's Memoirs and Letters: The Gospel of John, I, II, and III John*, vol. 4, Study Guide Commentary Series (Marshall, TX: Bible Lessons International, 1999).

25. The Police, "Every Breath You Take," by Sting. Originally released in 1983, track A on *Synchronicity* AMLX 63735, 45 rpm. A&M Records Ltd.

26. Mark Taylor, *Volume 28: 1 Corinthians*, New American Commentary: An Exegetical and Theological Exposition of Holy Scripture (Nashville: B&H Publishing, 2014), 408.

27. The line of logic here is informed by Stephen T. Um, *1 Corinthians: The Word of the Cross*, Preaching the Word Commentary Series (Wheaton, IL: Crossway, 2015), 277.

28. The distinction between the first Adam receiving life and the Second Adam imparting life was sourced from Mark Taylor, *Volume 28: 1 Corinthians*, 408, and Preben Vang, *1 Corinthians*, Teach the Text Commentary Series (Grand Rapids, MI: Baker Books, 2014), 215.

29. Um, *1 Corinthians: The Word of the Cross*, 276.

30. D. A. Carson, *The Gospel According to John*, The Pillar New Testament Commentary (Leicester, England; Grand Rapids, MI: Inter-Varsity Press; W. B. Eerdmans, 1991), 467–68.

31. Ben Witherington III, *The Gospel of Mark: A Socio-Rhetorical Commentary* (Grand Rapids, MI: William B. Eerdmans Publishing Company, 2001), 102–03.

32. James R. Edwards, *The Gospel According to Mark*, The Pillar New Testament Commentary (Grand Rapids, MI; Leicester, England: Eerdmans; Apollos, 2002).

33. Walter A. Elwell and Barry J. Beitzel, "Heart," in *Baker Encyclopedia of the Bible* (Grand Rapids, MI: Baker Book House, 1988), 1:938.

34. Madame Jeanne Guyon, *Experiencing God Through Prayer* (Springdale, PA: Whitaker House, 1984), 11.

35. Jan Johnson, *When the Soul Listens;* 2nd ed. (Colorado Springs, CO: NavPress, 2017), 35.

36. Larry Warner, *Journey with Jesus: Discovering the Spiritual Exercises of Saint Ignatius* (Downers Grove, IL: IVP Books, 2010), 28–31.

37. G. Chamberlain, "Refuge," *International Standard Bible Encyclopedia, Revised*, ed. Geoffrey W. Bromiley (Grand Rapids, MI: Wm. B. Eerdmans), 4:66.

38. Rodney L. Cooper, *Mark*, Holman New Testament Commentary, vol. 2 (Nashville, TN: Broadman & Holman Publishers, 2000).

39. Spiros Zodhiates, ed., *Hebrew-Greek Key Word Study Bible, NIV Edition* (Chattanooga, TN: AMG, 1996), 2,122.

40. William Hendriksen, *New Testament Commentary: Exposition of the Gospel According to Matthew* (Grand Rapids, MI: Baker Publishing Group, 1973), 516.

41. See these resources for more on the Greek word ἵστημι: https://www.studylight.org/lexicons/eng/greek/2476.html and https://biblehub.com/greek/2476.htm.

42. Charles Haddon Spurgeon, "Jesus Wept," *The Metropolitan Tabernacle Pulpit Sermons* (London: Passmore & Alabaster, 1889), 35:338. Italics in quote are author emphasis.

43. Arnold Dallimore, *Spurgeon: A New Biography* (Edinburgh, UK; Banner of Truth, 1987), 186.

44. Spurgeon, "Jesus Wept."

45. *Dictionary of the New Testament Background*, eds. C. A. Evans and S. E. Porter (Downers Grove, IL: Intervarsity Press, 2000), 1276–80.

46. Frederick Buechner, *Wishful Thinking* (San Francisco, CA: HarperOne, 1993).

47. Walter A. Elwell and Barry J. Beitzel, "Apostle, Apostleship," in *Baker Encyclopedia of the Bible* (Grand Rapids, MI: Baker Book House, 1988), 1:131.

48. Craig L. Blomberg, *Who Is Jesus of Nazareth* (Bellingham, WA: Lexham Press, 2021), 4.

49. Kenneth E. Bailey, *Jesus Through Middle Eastern Eyes* (Downers Grove, IL; IVP Academic, 2008), 95.

50. John Ashton, "Abba," *The Anchor Yale Bible Dictionary*, ed. David Noel Freedman (New York: Doubleday, 1992), 1:7.

51. Bailey, *Jesus Through Middle Eastern Eyes*, 91.

52. Hendriksen, *New Testament Commentary*, 184.

53. Hendriksen, *Exposition of the Gospel According to Luke*, 186.

54. Stuart K. Weber, *Matthew*, Vol. 1, Holman New Testament Commentary (Nashville, TN: Broadman & Holman Publishers, 2000).

55. Donald K. Campbell, "Foreword," in *Basic Bible Interpretation: A Practical Guide to Discovering Biblical Truth*, ed. Craig Bubeck Sr. (Colorado Springs, CO: David C. Cook, 1991), 101.

56. "There Is None Like You," lyrics by Don Moen, music by Lenny LeBlanc.

Check out some of Lisa's other great books!

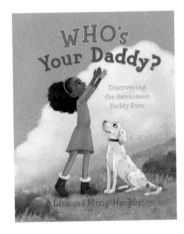

THE SACRAMENT OF HAPPY

Many think happiness is circumstantially-based, therefore "unspiritual", so it's a delight to tag along with Lisa as she dives deep into Scripture to prove otherwise!

LIFE

In her trademark blend of solid biblical teaching and relatable, humorous wit, Lisa Harper offers *LIFE*, a devotional that proves the gospel is ready and able to speak to your real-world, real-time, real-life issues, big or small.

WHO'S YOUR DADDY?

When someone asks Missy a big question—"Who's your daddy?"—she starts thinking and learning a lot about daddies, especially Daddy God, who loves us all unconditionally.

BIBLE STUDIES FROM LISA HARPER

7 Sessions

Discover divine love in the often overlooked and misunderstood passages in Scripture, and find that Jehovah of the Old Testament is the same God we see through Jesus Christ in the New Testament.

7 Sessions

Discover some radically redemptive facets of pain and suffering while you learn how to engage with and authentically embrace the wounded world around you through the unlikely hope and joy that permeate even the hardest moments in Job's story.

7 Sessions

Explore the action-packed Gospel of Mark—the first literary compilation of Jesus' earthly life and ministry—to lean further into His divine compassion in a way that might just change your life forever!

7 Sessions

Journey through the Book of Hebrews for an eye-opening and encouraging experience to help increase your intimacy with Jesus and deepen your faith in Him. He'll teach you not to falter when faced with personal difficulties or cultural persecution.

Available wherever books are sold.

Pricing and availability subject to change without notice.